THE REAL
YASUKE

HISTORY BEYOND THE SAMURAI MYTH

Dr. Alaric Naudé

The Real Yasuke: History Beyond the Samurai Myth

弥助:侍伝説の歴史学的検証

Copyright © 2024 by Dr. Alaric Naude 能出新陸 (のうで あらりく)

Published by United Scholars Academic Press (學者聯合學問出版社), Republic of Korea & Commonwealth of Australia

Paperback ISBN: 978-1-7637811-0-8

THANKS TO

Special thanks to:

Anthony S. PhD, 夢想神伝流居合道- 四段(Musō Shinden Ryū Iaidō - 4th dan) who gave me several suggestions and was kind enough to double check some terminology for me.

Prof. Jason W. Wellman – Applied Linguist who also looked over my work and gave some insights.

Oliver Jia, IR Researcher

Also to the many other professionals and advanced readers in Japan and other countries that provided thoughts and feedback.

TABLE OF CONTENTS

7

PREFACE

I have long been fascinated by the cultural and linguistic similarities and differences across East Asia. One of my areas of study focuses on understanding the cultural and linguistic interchange that has taken place in this region, leading me to develop a hypothesis on language continuity between Manchu (満洲語), Korean (韓国語), and Japanese (日本語). This interest naturally led me to investigate unique cultural exchanges and historical interactions, such as the story of Yasuke (弥助), the African retainer of Oda Nobunaga (織田信長). However, the more I delved into the narrative, the more confusion I encountered. With so many conflicting accounts, I decided to systematically analyze the available literature and historical records from various languages, including Portuguese, Chinese (中国語), Korean (韓国語), and Japanese (日本語), to determine if any critical information had been overlooked. Unsurprisingly, the most valuable sources came from Portuguese and Japanese documents, given the context of Nobunaga's Japan.

Researching the life of Yasuke (弥助) has been both challenging and rewarding. Very few primary documents provide a detailed account of his life, and the ones that do, such as records by Jesuit missionaries like Luís Fróis, are brief and vague. This scarcity of information has made it necessary to piece together fragments, which on their own are incomplete, leaving significant gaps in our understanding of who Yasuke was and how he navigated the complex world of 16th-century Japan.

As a professor of linguistics, I approach history not only through the lens of events but also through the language and culture that shape the way these events are recorded and understood. Language is deeply intertwined with the values and norms of the society in which it is used, and understanding Yasuke's life within the broader context of the Sengoku (戦国時代) and Azuchi-Momoyama periods (安土桃山時代) requires a nuanced understanding of the cultural and linguistic realities of that time.

This period is especially significant, as it laid the foundation for many of the conflicts that would later affect the broader East Asian region, including Korea and China. For instance, the Imjin War (1592–1598), which resulted from Toyotomi Hideyoshi's invasions of Korea, was a direct outgrowth of the power struggles from the Azuchi-Momoyama period (安土桃山時代). The political and military developments during this era set the stage for cultural and linguistic interactions that would shape East Asia for centuries. These events had a profound impact on language evolution, diplomatic relations, and the way history was recorded across the region.

In writing this book, my goal has been to follow the evidence as faithfully as possible, while also placing Yasuke's life within its proper cultural and linguistic context. It would be a disservice to the pursuit of historical truth to romanticize or embellish the facts. While such an approach may be the realm of fiction writers, historians and social scientists are bound by their responsibility to present an accurate portrayal of the past, based on evidence.

This book is not an attempt to craft a fictional narrative where there is none, nor does it seek to fill in the gaps with speculative tales. Instead, I have tried to situate Yasuke's experience within the larger historical framework of Azuchi-Momoyama Japan, examining how foreigners were perceived, what roles they played in society, and how Nobunaga's court functioned during a time of great upheaval. By grounding Yasuke's story in the realities of the 16th century, I hope to offer a clearer understanding of his position in Japanese history and the significant cultural and linguistic changes that were beginning to unfold at the time.

Understanding history as accurately as possible is more than an academic pursuit; it is a commitment to honoring the truth of the past. While much about Yasuke remains a mystery, I have endeavored to present what can be reasonably known, free from distortion or myth, so that readers can appreciate his extraordinary story within the complex and fascinating world of 16th-century

Japan—a world that would continue to shape the region for centuries to come.

AZUCHI-MOMOYAMA PERIOD (安土桃山時代)

The Azuchi-Momoyama period (安土桃山時代) and the Sengoku period (戦国時代) are closely related phases in Japanese history, with the former marking the conclusion of the latter. Understanding their connection helps clarify the significant social, political, and military changes that Japan underwent during the 16th century.

THE SENGOKU PERIOD (戦国時代): A TIME OF CONSTANT WARFARE

The Sengoku period, also known as the Warring States period, spanned roughly from the mid-15th century (around 1467) to the late 16th century (around 1573). It was a time of intense political fragmentation, social upheaval, and nearly constant military conflict between rival daimyō (大名), the regional warlords who ruled Japan's provinces. The period began in the aftermath of the Ōnin War (応仁の乱), a civil war that broke out in Kyoto in 1467, which left the central authority of the Ashikaga shogunate (足利幕府) severely weakened. With the shogunate's decline, local daimyō

19

began vying for power, often engaging in warfare to expand their territories and assert dominance over one another.

During the Sengoku period, the traditional feudal hierarchy broke down, and Japan was divided into competing territories, each controlled by a daimyō who commanded armies of samurai (侍) and ashigaru (足軽, foot soldiers). Social mobility became more fluid during this time, as military success on the battlefield could elevate individuals of non-samurai background into positions of power. The Sengoku period is characterized by a lack of central authority, a continuous struggle for supremacy, and the rise of powerful warlords such as Oda Nobunaga (織田 信長), Toyotomi Hideyoshi (豊臣 秀吉), and later Tokugawa Ieyasu (徳川 家康).

TRANSITION TO THE AZUCHI-MOMOYAMA PERIOD (安土桃山時代)

The Azuchi-Momoyama period refers to the final years of the Sengoku period, spanning from approximately 1573 to 1600. It is named after the Azuchi Castle (安土城) built by Oda Nobunaga and Momoyama Castle (桃山城) built by Toyotomi Hideyoshi. This period represents the final efforts to unify Japan under a central authority after over a century of civil war.

While the Sengoku period is characterized by widespread instability and disunity, the Azuchi-Momoyama period marks the time when powerful warlords—especially Oda Nobunaga and Toyotomi Hideyoshi—began to consolidate power and bring the fragmented provinces of Japan under centralized rule. Both Nobunaga and Hideyoshi were pivotal in ending the long-standing conflicts of the Sengoku period by defeating or subduing rival daimyō and implementing new administrative and social reforms to stabilize the country.

At the heart of these dramatic changes was Oda Nobunaga (織田信長), one of the most ambitious and ruthless warlords of the time. Nobunaga, the daimyō of Owari Province (尾張国), was not content with regional power; he sought nothing less than the complete unification of Japan under his rule. Known for his revolutionary military strategies, Nobunaga was among the first to embrace the use of firearms, specifically the arquebus (火縄銃), [1]which had been introduced to Japan by Portuguese traders in the

---

[1] The term arquebus is derived from the Dutch word *Haakbus*, which translates to "hook gun." This name originally referred to a type of firearm used from the 15th to the 17th centuries. The defining feature of the *Haakbus* was a hook-like projection or lug on its underside, which allowed the user to brace the gun against battlements, walls, or other sturdy surfaces for stability when firing. This design feature was necessary due to the substantial recoil and the weight of the early firearms. The *arquebus* evolved over time, and its matchlock firing mechanism became closely associated with the weapon (hence sometimes being called a matchlock gun). This mechanism allowed for a slow-burning match to ignite the gunpowder, making the arquebus one of the earliest firearms to use a mechanical ignition system rather than manual lighting. This innovation helped improve the practicality and effectiveness of firearms in warfare.

mid-16th century. With these weapons, combined with his disciplined infantry and aggressive tactics, Nobunaga was able to crush many of his rivals, including the mighty Takeda clan (武田氏) in the famous Battle of Nagashino (長篠の戦い) in 1575.

Nobunaga's rise to power was swift and brutal. In 1573, he overthrew the Ashikaga shogunate (足利幕府), ending the rule of the Ashikaga family, which had dominated Japanese politics since the 14th century. With the collapse of the shogunate, Nobunaga set his sights on building a unified Japan, constructing Azuchi Castle (安土城) near Kyoto (京都), a symbol of his dominance and his vision for a centralized government.

Yet Nobunaga's quest for power was not uncontested. Japan, at the time, was divided into many fiefdoms, each controlled by a daimyō with their own ambitions. Among his most notable rivals was Takeda Shingen (武田 信玄),[2] the fearsome daimyō of Kai Province (甲斐国), renowned for his cavalry and military prowess. For years, Shingen's Takeda clan was a major obstacle to Nobunaga's expansion, until Shingen's death in 1573, which opened the path for Nobunaga's conquests.

---

[2] 萩原, 三雄 (1988). *戦国武将武田信玄*. 新人物往来社.

Another significant figure was Uesugi Kenshin (上杉 謙信),[3] the warlord of Echigo Province (越後国), known for his skill in battle and his rivalry with both Nobunaga and Takeda Shingen. Although Kenshin and Nobunaga fought several times, notably during the sieges and skirmishes of the Kawanakajima (川中島の戦い) campaigns, Kenshin's sudden death in 1578 left Nobunaga with one fewer rival.

While Nobunaga pushed for unification in central Japan, other daimyō continued to exert their influence. One such figure was Mōri Motonari (毛利 元就),[4] who controlled much of western Honshu and held considerable naval power. The Mōri clan, known for its dominance over the Inland Sea (瀬戸内海), posed a threat to Nobunaga's expansion westward. Nobunaga would eventually clash with the Mōri clan in his quest to bring all of Japan under his control, particularly during the siege of Takamatsu (高松城の戦い).[5]

---

[3] 今福, 匡 (2018). *上杉謙信「義の武将」の激情と苦悩*. 星海社.

[4] 毛利博物館 (2007). *毛利元就と地域社会*. 山口県: 毛利博物館.

[5] Turnbull, S. (2013). *The Samurai: A Military History*. Tokyo: Tuttle Publishing.

However, it wasn't just rival warlords that Nobunaga had to contend with. The powerful and wealthy Buddhist sects (仏教勢力), particularly those at Mount Hiei (比叡山) and within the Ikkō-ikki (一向一揆) movement, represented another significant challenge to his authority. These militant monks, often aligned with local daimyō, commanded large armies and resisted Nobunaga's efforts to dominate the region. In response, Nobunaga employed ruthless tactics to suppress these religious groups, culminating in the infamous burning of Mount Hiei in 1571, where thousands of monks and civilians were massacred.

Despite these challenges, by 1582, Nobunaga had solidified his power across much of Japan, with only a few remaining regions resisting his rule. His dominance, however, would come to an abrupt and dramatic end during the Honnō-ji Incident (本能寺の変), when one of his own generals, Akechi Mitsuhide (明智 光秀), betrayed and attacked him. Nobunaga, caught off guard, was forced to commit seppuku (切腹), ritual suicide, marking the end of his reign and a major turning point in the Azuchi-Momoyama period.

In the wake of Nobunaga's death, his ambitious general, Toyotomi Hideyoshi (豊臣 秀吉), quickly moved to avenge his fallen lord and claim leadership over Nobunaga's vast territories. Hideyoshi, rising from humble beginnings as a common foot soldier, soon demonstrated his military brilliance and political acumen. He defeated Akechi Mitsuhide at the Battle of Yamazaki (山崎の戦い), consolidating his power and continuing Nobunaga's mission of unification.[6]

Toyotomi Hideyoshi's rise would mark the latter half of the Azuchi-Momoyama period. Unlike Nobunaga, Hideyoshi succeeded in bringing almost all of Japan under his control, even embarking on ambitious projects such as the invasion of Korea.[7] His influence on Japan was profound, particularly in terms of social and military reforms, which paved the way for the eventual establishment of the Tokugawa shogunate (徳川幕府).

Thus, the Azuchi-Momoyama period, though short, was a pivotal time in Japanese history. It was marked by the fierce ambitions of powerful daimyō like Oda Nobunaga and Toyotomi Hideyoshi, the fall of long-established political institutions, and the gradual unification of a war-torn nation. This was the Japan that Yasuke (弥助) found himself in when he arrived in 1581, a land where the

---

[6] Frois, L. (1976). *The First European Description of Japan, 1585: A Critical English-Language Edition of Striking Contrasts in the Customs of Europe and Japan*. (J. L. C. Boxer, Trans.). London: Routledge.

[7] Cartwright, M. (2019, June 05). Toyotomi Hideyoshi. *World History Encyclopedia/*

balance of power was continually shifting, and where a foreigner like him could become a notable figure in the court of a daimyō.

During the Azuchi-Momoyama period (安土桃山時代), Japan's interactions with the outside world were limited but significant. Most notably, the country had sporadic contact with European powers and traders through Portuguese, Spanish, and Jesuit missionaries, as well as longstanding regional connections with its immediate neighbors, China and Korea. These interactions with foreigners shaped Japan's understanding of the broader world, although Japan's worldview was still largely centered on East Asia, with China and Korea playing pivotal roles in its geopolitical thinking.

JAPAN'S CONTACT WITH THE WEST

The first direct contact Japan had with the West came in 1543, when Portuguese traders arrived on the island of Tanegashima (種子島). This encounter, during the Sengoku period (戦国時代), marked the beginning of a new era of trade and cultural exchange with European nations. The Portuguese brought with them new technologies, most notably the arquebus (火縄銃), which revolutionized Japanese warfare. Nobunaga (織田 信長), always quick to adopt military innovations, embraced the use of firearms, which became a decisive factor in his military campaigns.[8]

In addition to trade, the Portuguese also introduced Christianity to Japan through the efforts of Jesuit missionaries like Francis Xavier (フランシスコ・ザビエル), who arrived in Japan in 1549. Nobunaga himself was relatively tolerant of the missionaries, seeing them as potential allies against the Buddhist sects (仏教勢力), which he viewed as threats to his authority. Nobunaga allowed the Jesuits to preach and build churches in his domain, but he never converted to Christianity himself, using the missionaries more for political and strategic purposes than for religious conviction.

While Japan was open to these limited contacts with Europeans, its worldview remained largely centered on its relationships with China and Korea, two nations with which it had historical, cultural, and political ties dating back centuries. Japan's interactions with the West were still relatively peripheral in comparison to its deep-rooted relationships with its East Asian neighbors.

---

[8] Oka, M. (2022). The Origin of the Namban Trade: The Sea of Private Traders. In: Oka, M. (eds) War and Trade in Maritime East Asia. Palgrave Studies in Comparative Global History. Palgrave Macmillan, Singapore. https://doi.org/10.1007/978-981-16-7369-6_4

At the time of Oda Nobunaga, China was under the rule of the Ming dynasty (明朝), which had been established in 1368 and lasted until 1644. The Ming emperor contemporary to Nobunaga was the Wanli Emperor (万暦帝, 1572–1620), whose reign was marked by a mix of internal consolidation and external challenges.[9]

China under the Ming dynasty was the dominant power in East Asia, exerting significant cultural and political influence over Japan, Korea, and other neighboring states. Japan viewed China as the central force in the region, and while direct diplomatic relations between Japan and China had been sporadic due to piracy and political tensions, China remained the model for much of Japan's bureaucracy, art, and philosophy.

From Japan's perspective, China was not just a neighboring state but a civilizational center. The concept of Sinocentrism (中華思想), where China was seen as the "Middle Kingdom" surrounded by lesser tributary states, was deeply embedded in East Asian diplomacy. Japan's rulers, including Nobunaga, were well aware of China's power and influence, but they were also keen on

---

[9] 曹国庆. (1994). *万历皇帝大传*. 辽宁教育出版社.

asserting their own independence and distinctiveness from Chinese dominance.[10]

By Nobunaga's time, Japan had been indirectly influenced by China through trade and the exchange of ideas during the Kamakura period but gaining prominence during Sengoku, even though official relations between the two countries had fluctuated. As warlords sought legitimacy for their rule, they adopted Confucian values such as loyalty (忠, *chū*) and filial piety (孝, *kō*) to underpin social hierarchies and governance. Additionally, the concept of the Mandate of Heaven (天命, *tenmei* in Japanese) was adapted by Sengoku rulers to explain and legitimize their rise to power during a period of extreme social upheaval. The gekokujo (下克上)—the overthrow of superiors by inferiors—mirrored similar dynamics in Chinese history, where shifts in power were seen as natural under this doctrine Nobunaga himself, while ambitious and focused on unifying Japan, did not pursue significant direct relations with China, as his primary concerns were internal. However, China's centrality in the Japanese worldview remained unshaken, even as European traders and missionaries began to make their presence felt.

---

[10] Sakamoto, T. , Latz, . Gil , Watanabe, . Akira , Hijino, . Shigeki , Masamoto, . Kitajima , Notehelfer, . Fred G. , Hurst, . G. Cameron , Masai, . Yasuo , Toyoda, . Takeshi and Jansen, . Marius B. (2024, September 19). *Japan. Encyclopedia Britannica.* https://www.britannica.com/place/Japan

Japan's relationship with Korea was similarly complex. During Nobunaga's time, Korea was ruled by the Joseon dynasty (朝鮮王朝), which had been established in 1392 and would last until 1897. The Joseon king contemporary to Nobunaga was Seonjo (宣祖, r. 1567–1608). Like China, Korea was deeply influenced by Confucian thought and maintained a tributary relationship with the Ming dynasty.

While Korea and Japan had a long history of cultural exchange, including the transmission of Buddhism (仏教), Confucianism (儒教), and various technologies, relations were often tense due to piracy and territorial disputes. Japanese wakō (倭寇) pirates frequently raided the Korean coast, which led to diplomatic friction between the two countries. Despite these tensions, trade and diplomatic missions between Korea and Japan continued during this period, and both nations maintained a degree of mutual respect and cultural exchange.[11]

Nobunaga's reign did not see a major shift in relations with Korea, as his focus was primarily on consolidating power within Japan.[12]

---

[11] 장혜진. (2020). 일본 전국시대의 포르투갈 동아시아 교역과 일본 예수회의 선교활동. 동아시아고대학, (57), 109-134.

[12] 구태훈. (2008). 임진왜란 전의 일본사회—전국시대 연구 서설—. 사림, (29), 235-258.

However, his successor, Toyotomi Hideyoshi (豊臣 秀吉), would later attempt to expand Japanese influence over Korea through military force. Hideyoshi's invasions of Korea in 1592 and 1597—known as the Imjin War (壬辰倭乱)—were catastrophic for both Korea and Japan, severely straining relations and causing significant devastation to the Korean Peninsula.

During Nobunaga's lifetime, however, Korea was viewed as an important, though secondary, neighbor in comparison to China. Korea's Confucian bureaucracy and its tributary relationship with the Ming dynasty reinforced its position in the East Asian diplomatic order, and Japan, while aware of Korea's importance, was more focused on internal consolidation than expansion into Korean territory.

THE WORLD OF THE 16TH CENTURY

During the 16th century, Africa, Europe, and Asia were connected by a vast and complex network of trade routes and diplomatic interactions that spanned across oceans and continents. These connections were driven by the emergence of maritime powers in Europe, the flourishing of transcontinental trade in Asia, and Africa's strategic role in facilitating both trade and diplomacy. The primary catalysts for this global interaction were the Age of Exploration, initiated by European nations, and the establishment of trade empires that linked regions previously only connected through overland routes such as the Silk Road.

AFRICA'S ROLE IN GLOBAL TRADE

Africa, particularly along its coasts, played a significant role in the global trade network. Coastal regions in East and West Africa became central points of interaction between European, Arab, and Asian traders. The Swahili Coast (Eastern Africa), for example, had long been involved in trade with the Indian Ocean world, interacting with traders from India, Persia, and Arabia. By the 16th century, Portuguese explorers and traders had entered the scene, establishing fortified trading posts along the African coasts, such as Mozambique and Mombasa.[13]

The Portuguese, under explorers like Vasco da Gama, sought to control the lucrative Indian Ocean trade routes by linking Europe directly to Asia and Africa via the Cape of Good Hope.[14] They set up a network of trading posts along the African coastline, which facilitated the exchange of goods such as gold, ivory, and slaves in exchange for European goods and Asian luxury items like silk and spices. This integration of African coastal states into the global trading system had a profound impact on Africa's economy and also laid the groundwork for the later transatlantic slave trade.

Europe's Maritime Expansion

In Europe, the Age of Exploration fundamentally reshaped global interactions. Portuguese and Spanish explorers were at the forefront of this expansion. The Portuguese, led by figures like Prince Henry the Navigator, established the first European sea route

---

[13] Kollman, P. (2024). Catholic Missions and African Responses I: 1450–1800. In *The Palgrave Handbook of Christianity in Africa from Apostolic Times to the Present* (pp. 193-205). Cham: Springer International Publishing.

[14] Da Gama, V. (2009). Em nome de Deus: the journal of the first voyage of Vasco da Gama to India, 1497-1499. In *Em nome de Deus: The Journal of the First Voyage of Vasco da Gama to India, 1497-1499*. Brill.

to Asia via the southern tip of Africa.[15] This opened direct access to Asian markets for European traders, reducing their dependence on overland routes controlled by Ottoman and Persian intermediaries.

Spain, on the other hand, embarked on its own maritime ventures, famously resulting in Christopher Columbus' voyages to the Americas. However, the Spanish were also active in the Asian trade network, particularly after the establishment of the Manila-Acapulco galleon trade in the late 16th century, which connected Spanish-controlled territories in the Philippines to markets in both the Americas and Europe.[16]

This European maritime expansion led to an unprecedented era of global commerce. European ships traversed the Indian Ocean, bringing precious metals from the Americas to trade for Asian goods such as silk, porcelain, and spices. Diplomatic missions were also undertaken to establish treaties and trading rights with Asian powers, such as the Ming Dynasty (明朝) in China and the Mughal Empire (مغلیہ سلطنت) in India.

Asia's Economic and Diplomatic Networks

---

[15] Russell, P. E. (2019). Prince Henry the Navigator. In *The European Opportunity* (pp. 100-129). Routledge.

[16] Schwaller, J. F. (2016). Manila-Acapulco Galleon Trade. *The Spanish Empire: A Historical Encyclopedia [2 volumes]*, 95.

Asia, particularly through its empires like the Ming Dynasty in China, the Mughal Empire in India, and the various Sultanates of Southeast Asia, was a key player in global trade during the 16th century. The Silk Road remained a vital overland route, though it was increasingly complemented by maritime trade in the Indian Ocean.

China under the Ming Dynasty was the dominant economic power in East Asia, with its demand for silver—particularly from Japan and the Spanish Americas—driving global trade. Chinese merchants and diplomats interacted with both Southeast Asian kingdoms and European traders. Portuguese traders, who established the trading port of Macau (澳门) in 1557, were granted special privileges to trade directly with China, further linking Asian markets with European demand.[17]

India, under the rule of the Mughals, was another significant player in global trade, exporting textiles, spices, and gemstones. European powers such as Portugal and, later, the Dutch and British, established trading outposts in Indian coastal cities like Goa and Calicut to secure their share of this lucrative trade. Indian merchants

[17] Cartwright, M. (2021). Macau Portuguesa. *traduzido em português por Joana Mota. World History Encyclopedia em português, 21.*

also played a role in linking Africa, the Middle East, and Southeast Asia through established networks in the Indian Ocean.[18]

The Diplomatic Dimensions of Trade

Diplomatic relations were as important as trade in maintaining the stability and expansion of these global networks. The Portuguese were among the first European nations to establish formal diplomatic relations with both African and Asian rulers. In Ethiopia, the Portuguese formed an alliance with the Christian kingdom to support their war against Muslim forces, illustrating the intertwining of religion and diplomacy in these early contacts.

In Asia, Jesuit missionaries like Matteo Ricci were instrumental in establishing diplomatic relations with the Ming court in China. The Jesuits acted as intermediaries, bringing European knowledge of science and technology to Asia while advocating for trade rights and privileges for European powers. Diplomatic missions were also sent from Spain and Portugal to the Mughal and Ming courts to establish treaties that would facilitate more open trade.

During the Azuchi-Momoyama period (安土桃山時代), the presence of foreigners in Japan was an extraordinary rarity. The

---

[18] Subrahmanyam, S. (1993). *The Portuguese Empire in Asia, 1500-1700: A Political and Economic History*. Longman.

country had limited direct contact with the outside world, and the vast majority of foreigners encountered by the Japanese were either Chinese or Korean traders, and occasionally diplomats. Japan had long-standing trade and diplomatic relations with China and Korea, and these interactions were relatively familiar and regulated. However, individuals from more distant lands, such as Africa, India, or Europe, were almost entirely unknown, and to most Japanese people of the time, these "foreigners" were the stuff of myth and fairy tales.

CHINESE AND KOREAN TRADERS IN JAPAN

For centuries, Chinese and Korean traders had played a vital role in the flow of goods, culture, and knowledge to and from Japan. [19]These traders, operating within a broader East Asian trade network, brought goods such as silk (絹), porcelain (磁器), and medicinal herbs (薬草) to Japan. Trade with China was particularly significant, given that China, under the Ming dynasty (明朝), was the dominant power in the region. Japan's view of China was one

---

[19] Sakamaki, S. (1964). Ryukyu and Southeast Asia. The Journal of Asian Studies, 23(3), 383–389. doi:10.2307/2050757

of respect and emulation, with China being seen as a cultural center in East Asia. [20]

Similarly, Korea, had regular interactions with Japan, despite occasional tensions. Korean traders brought with them goods such as ginseng (人参), paper (紙), and textiles (織物). Diplomatic missions were also common between Japan and Korea, usually involving officials who were well-versed in each other's languages and customs. As a result, the Japanese people were relatively familiar with the appearance and customs of Chinese and Korean visitors, though they were still regarded with curiosity.

AFRICANS, INDIANS, AND OTHER DARK-SKINNED PEOPLES: THE "STUFF OF FAIRY TALES"

In contrast to Chinese and Korean visitors, individuals from more distant lands—particularly Africans, Indians, and other dark-skinned peoples—were entirely alien to most Japanese people during the Azuchi-Momoyama period. Knowledge of their existence came primarily from rumors, exaggerated tales, or second-hand reports from European traders and Jesuit missionaries. Such individuals were seldom seen in Japan, and for

---

[20] Chan, K. S. (2008). Foreign trade, commercial policies and the political economy of the song and Ming dynasties of China. *Australian Economic History Review, 48*(1), 68-90.

many Japanese, the idea that dark-skinned peoples even existed bordered on the fantastical.

Most information about these distant lands trickled into Japan through the Portuguese and later the Dutch, who had established trade routes and missionary outposts across Africa, India, and Southeast Asia.[21] These Europeans brought with them tales of the vast and exotic peoples they had encountered, including Africans, South Asians, and other groups unfamiliar to the Japanese. However, this information was slow to reach Japan and was often distorted by the time it arrived.

THE IMPACT OF JESUITS BRINGING AFRICANS OR INDIANS TO JAPAN

The arrival of Jesuit missionaries, such as Alessandro Valignano (アレッサンドロ・ヴァリニャーノ), in Japan in the late 16th century represented a major cultural shift. Valignano, a key figure in the Jesuit mission to Japan, brought with him not only European priests and scholars but also attendants and servants from places like India and Africa. Among these individuals was Yasuke (弥

---

[21] Goodman, G. K. (1955). *The Dutch Impact on Japan (1640-1853).* University of Michigan.

助), an African who would go on to serve Oda Nobunaga (織田 信長).

For the Japanese, encountering a man like Yasuke—likely the first African many had ever seen—caused a significant stir. Reports from Luís Fróis (ルイス・フロイス), a Jesuit missionary in Japan, describe the Japanese being astonished by Yasuke's dark skin, imposing height, and strength. Nobunaga himself was reportedly intrigued by Yasuke's appearance and even had him scrubbed to determine whether his skin color was natural or the result of ink or dye.[22] Such reactions underscore how utterly foreign and remarkable the appearance of an African man was in 16th-century Japan.

Similarly, if Jesuits had brought Indians or other dark-skinned individuals to Japan, the reaction would have been much the same. While the Japanese were not entirely isolated from the rest of the world, their interactions with foreigners were largely limited to East Asia. Thus, the arrival of people from the Indian subcontinent, Africa, or Southeast Asia was a momentous event, causing fascination and bewilderment among the local population.[23]

---

[22] Fróis, L. (1585). *História de Japam.*

CULTURAL IMPACT AND CURIOSITY

The appearance of dark-skinned foreigners in Japan also played into the broader sense of curiosity that Japanese leaders and commoners alike had about the wider world. Nobunaga, for instance, was known for his interest in foreign cultures, including Christianity and Western military technology, which the Jesuits had introduced. The arrival of people like Yasuke gave Nobunaga and his court an opportunity to engage directly with the global trade and diplomatic networks that were slowly beginning to touch Japan's shores.

However, this curiosity did not necessarily extend to broader Japanese society. For most ordinary people, foreigners—especially those from outside of East Asia—remained strange, distant figures. The appearance of someone like Yasuke would have fueled stories and legends about distant lands filled with mysterious and exotic peoples. Such encounters would have left a lasting impression on those who saw or heard of these visitors but had little to no impact on the daily lives of most.

A BROADER LOOK AT FOREIGNERS IN JAPAN

Later, we will explore how the presence of foreigners, particularly

Jesuit missionaries and their African or Indian attendants, impacted

Japan's political and cultural landscape during the Azuchi-Momoyama period.

These interactions set the stage for further, albeit limited, engagement between Japan and the broader world before Japan entered its self-imposed isolation under the Tokugawa shogunate (徳川幕府) in the 17th century.[24]

The rarity of foreign visitors in Japan, particularly those from Africa, India, or Southeast Asia, cannot be overstated. These encounters were rare enough to cause major intrigue and excitement among the Japanese, and they played a role in shaping the limited worldview that existed in Japan at the time.

 Despite fictitious claims that Japan was somehow involved in the African slave trade, Japan itself had no colonial ambitions in Africa, nor did it establish trading posts or settlements there. Unlike the Portuguese, who actively sought to exploit African labor in their colonies, Japan had no such system in place. Even after the arrival of European traders, Japan's interest lay in the acquisition of Western goods and military technology, rather than

---

[24] Ramesh, S., & Ramesh, S. (2020). The Tokugawa Period (1600–1868): Isolation and Change. *China's Economic Rise: Lessons from Japan's Political Economy*, 101-133.

the integration into European and Arab-controlled global slave markets.

JAPAN'S ISOLATIONIST POLICIES AND THE END OF FOREIGN INFLUENCE

Following the Azuchi-Momoyama period, Japan's interactions with foreign powers became even more restricted. Under the Tokugawa Shogunate (徳川幕府), which was established in 1603, Japan enacted a series of isolationist policies, culminating in the Sakoku (鎖国) edict of the 1630s.[25] These policies essentially sealed Japan off from nearly all foreign trade and diplomacy, with the exception of limited contacts with the Dutch at Dejima (出島) and controlled trade with China and Korea.

This period of isolation further confirms that Japan was not engaged in any form of African slave trading. While European powers, particularly the Portuguese and later the Dutch, were heavily involved in the global slave trade, Japan's self-imposed isolation ensured that the country did not become entangled in these networks.

---

[25] Naoko, I. (2013). Wei Zhiyan and the Subversion of the Sakoku. *Offshore Asia: Maritime Interactions in East Asia before Steamships*, 236-58.

ABSENCE OF EVIDENCE FOR JAPAN'S PARTICIPATION IN THE SLAVE TRADE

The idea that Japan participated in the African slave trade during the Azuchi-Momoyama period, or indeed during any period of its history, is not supported by historical documentation. In fact, no Japanese records or foreign sources indicate that Japan engaged in the buying or selling of African slaves. The presence of a few Africans or Indians brought to Japan by European traders or missionaries is a far cry from any systemic involvement in the global trade of enslaved people.

Scholarly works on Japanese foreign relations during the Sengoku (戦国時代) and Edo periods (江戸時代) focus on Japan's internal consolidation and its regional interactions with East Asia, with little emphasis on direct connections to African peoples or involvement in slavery. Even European accounts, such as those from Portuguese Jesuit missionaries or traders, do not document any Japanese involvement in the African slave trade.

YASUKE'S JOURNEY TO JAPAN

The origins of Yasuke (弥助) are surrounded by mystery and speculation due to a lack of historical records. While historical documents provide a glimpse into Yasuke's life in Japan, his origins and how he came to be in the company of the Jesuits (イエズス会) remain subjects of scholarly debate. Historical evidence, drawn from both Japanese and Jesuit sources, suggests that Yasuke may have come from Mozambique or elsewhere in East Africa, brought to Asia through the extensive Portuguese trading networks.

PLAUSIBLE ORIGINS OF YASUKE

Yasuke's African origins are often attributed to Mozambique, a Portuguese colony in Southeast Africa during the 16th century. Mozambique was a key node in the Portuguese Indian Ocean trade network, where enslaved people, as well as free Africans, were transported to India, Southeast Asia, and, in rare cases, to places as distant as Japan. Although the exact location of Yasuke's birth is unknown, it is reasonable to place him in East Africa, as the Portuguese had active trading posts and military outposts along the Swahili coast, including Mozambique Island.

Mozambique and the wider region of East Africa were integral to Portuguese colonial expansion. Here, the Portuguese engaged in trade, diplomacy, and slavery, which involved capturing people from the interior of Africa and sending them to Portuguese territories across the Indian Ocean. It is plausible that Yasuke, as a young man, could have been taken from this region either as an enslaved person or as a free African who entered service with the Portuguese.

Several Japanese sources and interpretations support the idea that Yasuke might have originated from this region. A prominent theory in Japanese literature is that Yasuke was a Makhua or a member of one of the Bantu-speaking groups inhabiting Mozambique. These theories, while plausible, remain speculative as there is no definitive record specifying Yasuke's exact ethnic background. It must be clearly understood by the reader however , that even the Mozambique theory is not attested to by historical records but rather on the speculation of historians based on the Portuguese activities in Africa and India. I repeat, there is no historical record of Yasuke's ethnicity or tribe.

HOW YASUKE CAME TO BE WITH THE JESUITS

Yasuke arrived in Japan as part of the entourage of Alessandro Valignano (アレッサンドロ・ヴァリニャーノ), an Italian Jesuit missionary who served as the Visitor (an inspector responsible for overseeing Jesuit missions) in the Portuguese East Indies. Valignano had traveled extensively throughout the Portuguese colonies in India, Southeast Asia, and Japan, organizing missionary activities and ensuring the success of Catholicism in Asia. It was during his travels to Goa (India)—a major hub in the Portuguese Empire—that Valignano likely encountered Yasuke.

There are a few possibilities as to how Yasuke came into Valignano's service:

1. Yasuke May Have Been a Slave: It is possible that Yasuke was originally enslaved by the Portuguese and brought to Goa or another Portuguese colony in Asia. The Portuguese were heavily involved in the Indian Ocean slave trade, and many Africans were brought to India to work as laborers or servants. Jesuit missionaries often traveled with African attendants, who may have been enslaved individuals purchased or inherited by the missionaries. In this case, Yasuke may have been acquired by Valignano in Goa or

Mozambique. The fact that the Portuguese gave him to Nobunaga may mean that he was still a slave to the Portuguese but that Nobunaga released him and gave him the status of a free servant since he was given a stipend.

2. Yasuke May Have Been Freed: Another possibility is that Yasuke was freed from slavery, either before or after entering Jesuit service. Some sources suggest that African slaves in Portuguese territories could sometimes buy their freedom or be granted it by their masters. Valignano, being a high-ranking Jesuit, might have freed Yasuke and brought him along on his journey as a trusted servant. In Japanese writings, this theory has been explored as part of the speculation around Yasuke's mysterious past.

3. Yasuke May Have Been a Free African: Alternatively, Yasuke could have been a free African who entered the service of the Jesuits voluntarily. During the 16th century, some Africans served as soldiers, mercenaries, or attendants in the Portuguese Empire, and it was not unheard of for free Africans to work for European or Portuguese employers. This theory posits that Yasuke might have been

a mercenary or a bodyguard who accompanied Valignano as part of his entourage. Jesuit sources occasionally mention the presence of African bodyguards who accompanied missionaries on their travels. This does seem unlikely though considering the language used to refer to him by the Jesuits.

JAPANESE LITERATURE ON YASUKE'S ORIGINS AND STATUS

Japanese historical records, such as those by Luis Fróis (ルイス・フロイス), a Jesuit priest who chronicled life in Japan, give us a firsthand account of Yasuke's arrival. Fróis described Yasuke's entry into Nobunaga's service and highlighted the novelty of an African man in Japan at the time. However, Fróis does not provide extensive details about Yasuke's life prior to his arrival in Japan, leaving much of his earlier life open to interpretation. The Jesuit Annual Report (イエズス会年報) written in Japan provides further glimpses into the daily activities of Jesuits, but again, details about Yasuke's origins are scarce.[26]

Japanese scholars have also looked into Yasuke's cultural significance, particularly his unique position as an African in 16th-century Japan. Records suggest that arrival of foreign individuals

---

[26] Fróis, L. (1585). *História de Japam*.

like Yasuke was seen as a sign of Japan's growing interaction with the world, but without suggesting that Yasuke's life reflected widespread Japanese engagement in slavery or human trafficking.

WAS YASUKE A SLAVE WHO BOUGHT HIS FREEDOM?

While it is possible that Yasuke was originally enslaved, there is no direct evidence to confirm whether he bought his freedom before arriving in Japan. The Jesuits did not usually participate directly in the slave trade, but they did have enslaved individuals in their service, especially in Portuguese colonies. However, some enslaved people under Jesuit control were eventually manumitted, and it is conceivable that Yasuke was freed either before or during his time with Valignano.

So, we are finally left with only possibilities and no real answers as to the social status of Yasuke at the time he met Nobunaga.

THE POWER OF NAMES

The introduction of Kanji (漢字) to Japan occurred during the Asuka period (飛鳥時代), which spanned from 538 to 710 CE. This was a pivotal time in Japanese history when many cultural, religious, and technological innovations from the Asian mainland, particularly from China (中国) and Korea (韓国), began to shape early Japanese society.

Kanji was first introduced to Japan from Baekje (百済), one of the Three Kingdoms of Korea (韓国三国時代), which included Silla (新羅), Goguryeo (高句麗), and Baekje. Baekje had strong diplomatic and cultural ties with both China and Japan.[27] It was via Baekje that Japan first received Chinese texts, including Buddhist scriptures, and was exposed to the Chinese writing system.

China's Tang dynasty (唐朝), which ruled from 618 to 907 CE, was also a significant influence. During the Nara period (奈良時

---

[27] 조진석. (2024). 백제의 한자 수용과 문서 행정 시기. 호서고고학, 38-62.

代), following the Asuka period, Japan continued to deepen its cultural ties with the Tang dynasty. The flourishing of diplomatic relations between Japan and China during this time further facilitated the introduction of Chinese characters to Japan, as the Japanese sent emissaries, known as Kentōshi (遣唐使), to the Tang court to study Chinese culture, religion, administration, and the writing system.[28]

Kanji, originally used to represent Chinese sounds and meanings, was adapted by the Japanese to represent their language. However, the syntax and grammar of Japanese differed greatly from Chinese, and this led to the development of man'yōgana (万葉仮名), an early script that used Chinese characters for their phonetic values to write Japanese.[29]

Hiragana (ひらがな) and Katakana (カタカナ) developed as phonetic scripts (Syllabaries), or kana (仮名), from Kanji (漢字) in Japan during the Heian period (平安時代), which spanned from 794 to 1185 CE. These scripts were created to better suit the Japanese language, as Kanji, with its Chinese origins, was not an

---

[28] 권인한. (2010). The Evolution of Ancient East Asian Writing Systems as Observed through Early Korean and Japanese Wooden Tablets. Korea Journal, 50(2), 124-157.

[29] 山田健三. (2013). 書記用語「万葉仮名」をめぐって. 人文科学論集 文化コミュニケーション学科編, 47, 15-30.

ideal fit for Japanese grammar and structure. The process by which each script developed is truly fascinating.

DEVELOPMENT OF HIRAGANA (ひらがな)

Hiragana originated from man'yōgana (万葉仮名), an early writing system that used Kanji purely for their phonetic value, rather than for their meaning. Hiragana evolved by simplifying and cursively writing certain Kanji characters. These simplified forms were easier to write and became particularly popular among women in the Heian court because they were traditionally not taught formal Kanji, which was used by men for official documents and literature.

In fact, Hiragana was sometimes called "onnade" (女手), meaning "women's hand," because of its use in personal correspondence, poetry, and diaries written by women. One of the most famous works in Hiragana is the "Tale of Genji" (源氏物語), written by the noblewoman Murasaki Shikibu (紫式部).

Over time, Hiragana became more widely used by both men and women, and it became the standard script for grammatical particles, verb endings, and native Japanese words for which there was no appropriate Kanji.

DEVELOPMENT OF KATAKANA (カタカナ)

Katakana also developed from man'yōgana, but in a different way. It originated from parts of Kanji characters, particularly by taking a fragment or radical of a Kanji and using it for its phonetic value. This script was created by Buddhist monks in the Heian period to annotate Chinese texts they were studying. They used Katakana as a form of shorthand to represent the sounds of Japanese words while reading and interpreting classical Chinese texts.[30]

Because it was used as a reading aid, Katakana was seen as a more formal and structured script, and it was associated with scholarly work, government documents, and foreign words. Over time, Katakana became the standard script used for foreign loanwords, onomatopoeia[31], and certain scientific or technical terms.[32]

DISTINCTION BETWEEN HIRAGANA AND KATAKANA

While both Hiragana and Katakana evolved from Kanji, they serve different functions in the modern Japanese writing system:

- Hiragana: Used for native Japanese words, grammatical functions (particles and verb endings), and for words that

---

[30] Miller, R. A. (1967). The Japanese Language.

[31] onomatopoeia is the formation of a word from a sound associated with what is named

[32] Seeley, C. (1991).A History of Writing in Japan.

do not have Kanji. It has a flowing, cursive style, which reflects its origins as a simplified version of Chinese characters.

- Katakana: Used for loanwords (words of foreign origin), onomatopoeia, names of plants, animals, and certain proper nouns. It has a more angular and sharp appearance, consistent with its origins as fragments of Kanji characters.

STANDARDIZATION AND MODERN USE

By the Meiji period (明治時代), Japan standardized the use of Hiragana and Katakana in conjunction with Kanji to create the modern Japanese writing system. Today, Hiragana is taught first to Japanese children because of its simplicity, while Katakana is typically introduced later for reading foreign words. Kanji is learned progressively due to its complexity, with a set number of characters taught in school as part of the official curriculum.

Thus, the development of Hiragana and Katakana helped to make the written Japanese language more accessible and better suited to the structure of native Japanese, allowing for a blend of Chinese influences and native phonetic representation.

Kanji (漢字) also plays a significant role in the naming traditions of China (中国), Korea (韓国), and Japan (日本) due to the deep semantic and cultural meanings embedded in each character.

Unlike many Western names, which are often chosen for their sound or familial connection, names in these East Asian cultures reflect social rank, aspirations, virtues, and the individual's state of existence. A name is not just a label; it conveys status, identity, and personal character. Here's an overview of how Kanji influences naming traditions in these three cultures:

KANJI IN CHINESE NAMING TRADITIONS (中国の名前)

In China, the use of Chinese characters (漢字) for names is deeply symbolic, as each character is chosen for its meaning as well as its sound. Typically, Chinese names consist of a surname (姓) and a given name (名), where the surname comes first.

Surnames: Chinese surnames are usually single-character, ancient, and tied to family lineage. They convey the individual's familial and social origins. There are only about a hundred common surnames in China, many of which are associated with noble families, historical figures, or important clans.

Given Names: These are often two characters, and each character holds significant meaning. Parents choose characters that reflect virtues (such as wisdom 智 or loyalty 忠), nature (such as mountain 山 or ocean 海), or aspirations (such as prosperity 富 or success 成). The combination of these characters is intended to shape the child's identity and destiny.

Social Rank and Name Changes: In Imperial China, names could change upon elevation in social rank or status. A scholar who passed the imperial exams and entered the scholar-official class might adopt a new name, reflecting his new status and role in society. For example, a name change might include characters symbolizing wisdom, service, or loyalty to the emperor, showcasing the person's elevated position.

The importance of Kanji in names can be seen in its strong semantic weight. A name like Wang Zhi (王智), where 王 means "king" or "monarch" and 智 means "wisdom," conveys an aspiration for royal wisdom, strength, and leadership.

KANJI IN KOREAN NAMING TRADITIONS (韓国の名前)

In Korea, Hanja (漢字, the Korean term for Chinese characters) was historically used for personal names and family names until the use of Hangul (한글) became widespread.

Surnames: Like China, Korean surnames tend to be single-character and are deeply tied to familial lineage. Korean surnames are fewer in number but hold significant weight in terms of ancestry. Names like Kim (金) or Lee (李) are extremely common, but the specific clan or bon-gwan (本貫) is crucial, as it shows the individual's ancestral village or family origin.

Given Names: Korean given names typically consist of two Hanja characters, where each character holds meaning. For instance, a name like Jin-ho (振浩), where 振 means "to flourish" and 浩 means "vastness," can represent a desire for the individual to thrive and have great influence.

Name Changes and Social Rank: In Korean history, name changes were common when an individual rose in rank or earned a significant title. The new name would reflect the virtues or roles associated with their new station. For example, kings and scholars often adopted posthumous names (諡號, 시호) to reflect their accomplishments and virtues. These posthumous names were chosen to embody the ideal characteristics of the individual's life.

Hanja-based names thus go beyond sound; they signify the individual's identity, virtues, and place in society, reflecting aspirations and expectations.

KANJI IN JAPANESE NAMING TRADITIONS (日本の名前)

In Japan, Kanji characters play an equally important role in social identity and personal meaning. A Japanese name typically consists of a surname (名字 or 姓) and a given name (名), both written in Kanji. The meaning of the Kanji chosen for a person's name is crucial in defining their character, aspirations, and status.

- Surnames: Japanese surnames are typically composed of two Kanji characters, and the meaning often reflects geographical features or natural elements related to the family's origin. For example, the surname Yamada (山田) means "mountain field," indicating the family's connection to agricultural land or mountainous regions.

- Given Names: Parents carefully select characters for given names to express their hopes for their child's future. For example, the name Takechiyo (竹千代), which was the childhood name of Tokugawa Ieyasu, combines the character 竹 (take), meaning bamboo, a symbol of strength and endurance, with 千代 (chiyo), which signifies a thousand generations. Together, the name expresses the wish for longevity and resilience, much like the strong, flexible bamboo that endures through the ages. Similarly, the childhood name Bontenmaru (梵天丸) of Date Masamune was chosen with a specific intention. 梵 (bon) refers to Brahma, a deity symbolizing protection and strength, and 天 (ten) means heaven, while 丸 (maru), often used in boys' names, suggests completeness or strength. The combination of these characters conveys a hope that the child will grow up strong, protected, and capable of great achievements under divine guidance. Through such thoughtful naming, parents project their deepest wishes and aspirations onto their children.of beauty and fleeting life in Japanese culture.

- Name Changes and Social Rank: Historically, as in China, name changes in Japan could occur upon promotion in rank or achievement of a title. A samurai who was elevated in status by his daimyō could receive a new name, often with the character nobu (信, "faith" or "loyalty") or mitsu (光, "light" or "radiance") to reflect his new standing. Similarly, Buddhist monks often adopted new names upon entering the monastic life, with characters that conveyed spiritual enlightenment or humility.

Kanji names in Japan are deeply tied to an individual's existence and destiny. For example, in the Edo period (江戸時代), commoners and samurai alike had their names altered depending on their social mobility or as a result of marriage, service to a lord, or religious dedication.

THE SEMANTIC POWER OF KANJI IN NAMES

Kanji carries layers of meaning beyond phonetics, and this is what makes names in China, Korea, and Japan so much more than mere identifiers. Each character has its own meaning and can represent:

- Virtues (仁: "benevolence", 勇: "bravery"),
- Nature (山: "mountain", 海: "sea"),

- Wishes for the individual (福: "blessing", 富: "wealth").

Additionally, family status, aspirations, and cultural ideals are embedded in the chosen characters. A name change is not just a symbolic gesture but can indicate a transformation of one's social rank, personal status, or even life direction. For instance, receiving a name with the Kanji for "loyalty" (忠) upon being elevated to a samurai or official rank implies a strong connection to the values that person is now expected to uphold.[33]

The Semantics of Yasuke

The name 弥助 (Yasuke), while carrying meanings related to service and assistance, is indeed unlikely to have been the name of a warrior or someone of independent standing such as a 侍 (samurai). Let's examine why, by focusing more closely on the semantics and cultural connotations of the kanji.

---

[33] 金子哲. (2003). 中世後期民衆のサムライ観: 戦国期の多様な侍と王権の姿: 戦国期の多様な侍と王権の姿. 동북아시아문화학회 국제학술대회 발표자료집, 39-44.

ANALYSIS OF THE NAME "弥助"

弥 (み or や): The kanji 弥 can be read as "mi" or "ya," depending on the context. It has several meanings, including "increasing," "extending," or "to become more." This kanji is not commonly used in modern Japanese, but it is often seen in names or classical texts.

COMPONENTS:

Radical: 弓 (yumi) – The left component of the kanji 弥 is the radical 弓, which means "bow" (as in an archer's bow). This radical suggests an idea of stretching or extension, which can symbolically relate to the meaning of "increasing" or "expanding."

Right component: 尔 (ji) – The right side of 弥 is 尔 (ji), which primarily serves a phonetic role in this character. It doesn't directly contribute to the meaning but helps with the pronunciation of the kanji.

SEMANTICS:

In classical texts or names, 弥 often conveys a sense of continuation, growth, or something that extends over time.

助 (すけ)

助 is read as "suke" and means "to help" or "assist." It is a more commonly used character in Japanese, often appearing in names as well as in the word 助ける (tasukeru), which means "to help" or "save."

Radical: The radical is 力 (chikara), meaning "strength" or "power." This radical provides a clue to the meaning of 助, as it often appears in kanji related to physical strength, assistance, or action.

Right component: The right side is 且 (so), which serves as a phonetic element. It does not directly contribute to the meaning but complements the sound of the character.[34]

As mentioned earlier, this kanji carries connotations of "continuity" or "increasing" over time. While this could be seen as a positive attribute in terms of loyalty or endurance, it doesn't have the aggressive, martial, or heroic connotations that might be expected in the name of a warrior.

---

[34] Friday, K. F. (2004). *Samurai, warfare and the state in early medieval Japan*. Routledge.

WHY "弥助" IS UNLIKELY AS A WARRIOR NAME

Now some may rightly point out that both 弥 and 助 do appear in samurai names, however, understanding the key components of naming traditions —諱 (imina), 通称 (tsūshō), and 幼名 (yōmyō)—is essential, particularly in the context of the samurai class.

諱 (IMINA / KAIMYŌ)

The 諱 (imina) was a personal or posthumous name, typically kept private during one's lifetime and used primarily in formal or religious contexts. It carried great respect, often avoided in casual conversation, and was typically granted during the coming-of-age ceremony. For instance, in the case of 織田信長 (Oda Nobunaga), "信長" was his 諱. Additionally, 諱 played a role in Buddhist posthumous naming practices, where a new name was given after death to prevent the continued use of the earthly name.[35]

通称 (TSŪSHŌ)

The 通称 (tsūshō) was a commonly used name for everyday interactions, often based on birth order or other familial roles. For

---

[35] Loveday, L. (2019). Onomastic Configurations within Japanese Shintoism. *Onomastics between Sacred and Profane*, 91.

THE POWER OF NAMES

example, in 織田三郎平朝臣信長, "三郎" (Saburō) signifies his status as the third son, functioning as his 通称. Unlike the formal 諱, the 通称 was more flexible and could change throughout life, serving as a casual identifier compared to the reverence given to the 諱.[36]

幼名 (YŌMYŌ)

The 幼名 (yōmyō) was a childhood name given during youth and discarded upon reaching adulthood, often at the genpuku (coming-of-age) ceremony. A well-known example is 豊臣秀吉 (Toyotomi Hideyoshi), whose childhood name was 日吉丸 (Hiyoshi-maru). This informal name was used within the family or in early life until a more formal name was adopted.

THE CASE OF 弥助 (YASUKE)

Yasuke (弥助), who served Oda Nobunaga, presents a unique case in Japanese naming conventions. It is unclear whether "Yasuke" was his yōmyō, tsūshō, or an adopted name. Since Yasuke lacked both a surname and a 諱, it implies that he was not fully recognized as a samurai within the traditional hierarchy and that he

---

[36] 신종대. (2018). 무사의 이름체계 연구: 메이지 전후, 무사의 실명 (實名) 과 통칭 (通稱) 을 중심으로: 메이지 전후, 무사의 실명 (實名) 과 통칭 (通稱) 을 중심으로. 동북아 문화연구, 54, 111-127.

was a servant. In samurai society, having a 諱 was often a mark of noble status, and its absence suggests that Yasuke was outside this structure. Though "Yasuke" may function similarly to a tsūshō in daily usage, it doesn't carry the same formal weight as the names typically granted to those integrated into the samurai class.

In Oda Nobunaga's case:

- 織田 (Oda): Family name (氏).
- 信長 (Nobunaga): 諱, formal name after adulthood.
- 三郎 (Saburō): 通称, indicating his position as the third son.
- 平朝臣 (Taira no Ason): Hereditary title linking the family to the Taira clan and the court.

KANJI USAGE IN SAMURAI NAMES

弥 (Ya) and 助 (Suke) were common kanji in samurai names. The kanji 弥 frequently appeared in 通称 such as 弥三郎 (Yasaburō) or 弥右衛門 (Yaemon), which could reflect birth order or familial roles. However, 弥 also appeared in 諱, such as in 實弥 (Sanemi), demonstrating its versatility.

Similarly, 助 (Suke) and its variants like 介 or 輔, which share the same sound and meaning, were common in samurai 通称. Names like 助三郎 (Sukesaburō) were typical among higher-ranking samurai, conveying formality and status.

THE CASE OF 弥助 REVISITED

Despite the frequent use of 弥 and 助 in traditional samurai names, the combination 弥助 (Yasuke) does not align with typical 通称 patterns seen among samurai. Instead, 弥助 appears more like a 幼名 or a name given to someone of lower social standing. This impression arises from its simplicity and lack of the embellishments typically associated with the names samurai. For example, names like 弥三郎 or 助三郎 are more complex and formal, befitting those of noble or middle-tier status, whereas 弥助 lacks this level of refinement.

Thus, 弥助 does not resonate as a formal samurai name but instead reflects a name given in early life or to someone outside the traditional samurai hierarchy. This fits Yasuke's foreign origin and ambiguous social status within the rigid Japanese class system.

Furthermore, Yasuke's name was not found in the Sōkenkō Bukkan (総見公武鑑),[37] a record of all the kosho (小姓) and retainers under Nobunaga nor on other lists[38]. This absence raises

---

[37] 浅井玄卜. (1634). 総見公武鑑.

[38] 谷口, 名. (2000). *信長の親衛隊: 戦国覇者の多彩な人材* (中公新書 1453). 中央公論新社.

doubts about whether even his position as a kosho was officially recognized.

THE DAIMYŌ NOBUNAGA

To understand why Oda Nobunaga took an interest in Yasuke, we must first understand what type of person Nobunaga was. Known for his unconventional approach to leadership, Nobunaga was a man who valued talent and loyalty over tradition and birthright. His willingness to break from the rigid norms of Japanese society allowed him to embrace foreign ideas, technologies, and individuals in ways that other daimyō did not. Nobunaga's pragmatic and often ruthless nature led him to seek out those who could serve his ambitions, regardless of their background, race, or nationality. This open-minded yet calculating personality provides important context for his interest in Yasuke, an African who was as unique in appearance as he was in skill.

EARLY LIFE AND RISE TO POWER

Oda Nobunaga (織田 信長) was born in 1534 in Owari Province (尾張国), an area that is present-day Aichi Prefecture (愛知県). He was born into the Oda clan (織田氏), a family of mid-tier daimyō (regional lords) who controlled a modest but strategically important territory. Nobunaga's father, Oda Nobuhide (織田 信秀), was the head of the Oda clan and governed Nagoya Castle (名古屋城). The Oda clan's primary duty was to protect the borders of Owari

Province from larger, more powerful neighbors such as the Imagawa (今川氏) and Saitō (斎藤氏) clans.[39]

Nobunaga's early life was marked by behavior that was seen as rebellious and eccentric. As a youth, he was given the nickname "Owari no Ōutsuke (尾張の大うつけ)," or "The Fool of Owari." This moniker reflected his disregard for traditional decorum and his penchant for acting in ways that were seen as highly unconventional for someone of his noble status. For instance, Nobunaga was known for his wild behavior, dressing in inappropriate clothing for formal occasions and associating with lower-class people. His peers and even his retainers questioned his suitability to lead the clan.

Despite his unorthodox conduct, Nobunaga possessed a keen intelligence and a strategic mind that would become evident as he matured. His early defiance of tradition was later viewed as part of his larger ability to think outside the constraints of feudal customs, which would play a significant role in his military and political strategies.

Consolidation of Power

The death of Nobunaga's father, Oda Nobuhide, in 1551 thrust Nobunaga into a leadership role while he was still in his late teens. As the head of the Oda clan, Nobunaga faced immediate

---

[39] Ota, G., Elisonas, J. S., & Lamers, J. P. (2011). Book I Ōta Izumi No Kami Composed This. And It Records The Life Of Lord Oda Danjō No Jō Nobunaga From Eiroku 11 [1568], The Year Of Earth Senior And The Dragon. In *The Chronicle of Lord Nobunaga* (pp. 116-127). Brill.

opposition, both from within his family and from external rivals. His most prominent internal rival was his younger brother, Oda Nobuyuki (織田信行), who challenged Nobunaga's leadership.

The Oda family was internally divided, and many senior retainers supported Nobuyuki, viewing him as a more suitable successor due to Nobunaga's erratic behavior. Nobunaga, however, moved quickly to eliminate his rivals and consolidate his power. He first neutralized threats within his family by defeating Nobuyuki in

a series of conflicts. In 1557, Nobuyuki attempted a coup against Nobunaga but was betrayed by one of his own supporters. Nobunaga, now in full control of the Oda clan, ordered his brother's execution, an action that marked his ruthlessness and determination to eliminate potential threats to his authority.

Once Nobuyuki was eliminated, Nobunaga set about strengthening his position in Owari Province by building strategic alliances and preparing for military campaigns against neighboring lords. His consolidation of power was marked by a mix of political maneuvering, ruthless eliminations of enemies, and military innovation.

By his early twenties, Nobunaga had established himself as the undisputed leader of the Oda clan and began to expand his influence beyond Owari. His first major external threat came from Imagawa Yoshimoto (今川義元), a powerful daimyō who sought to march his army through Owari on the way to capture Kyoto (京都) and assert dominance over the weakened Ashikaga Shogunate (足利幕府). In 1560, Nobunaga would face Imagawa at the Battle of Okehazama (桶狭間の戦い), a battle that would dramatically alter his status as a military leader.

2. MILITARY GENIUS AND RUTHLESSNESS

Oda Nobunaga was not only a bold and unconventional leader but also a military innovator who dramatically altered the nature of warfare in Japan during the Sengoku period (戦国時代). His military strategy incorporated new technologies and tactical innovations, allowing him to defeat much larger and better-established forces. One of his most significant contributions to military strategy was the early adoption of firearms and the introduction of Western-style fortifications, which he learned from contact with Portuguese traders and Jesuit missionaries. These innovations, combined with his strategic alliances, such as his partnership with Tokugawa Ieyasu (徳川 家康), helped him expand his territory and establish dominance over his rivals.

74

EARLY ADOPTION OF FIREARMS

Nobunaga is particularly noted for his pioneering use of arquebuses (early muskets) on the battlefield. The introduction of firearms in Japan, facilitated by Portuguese traders in the mid-16th century, was a turning point for Japanese warfare. Nobunaga quickly grasped the potential of these weapons, and rather than seeing them merely as an auxiliary tool, he integrated them into his core military strategy. By training large numbers of foot soldiers (ashigaru) in the use of firearms and organizing them into volley-firing formations, Nobunaga was able to maximize the impact of the slow-loading arquebuses, which had traditionally been seen as inefficient due to their long reload times.[40]

WESTERN-STYLE FORTIFICATIONS

Nobunaga also embraced Western-style fortifications. His castle at Azuchi (安土城) incorporated stone foundations and strategic defenses, a stark departure from the traditional Japanese wooden fortresses. This innovation reflected Nobunaga's understanding of the changing nature of warfare, where siege warfare was becoming more important. Nobunaga's castles were built not just as

---

[40] Richardson, M. (2011). TEPPO AND SENGOKU: THE ARQUEBUS IN 16TH CENTURY JAPAN. *CONCORD REVIEW*, 187.

residences but as fortified military centers, capable of withstanding prolonged attacks.

FAMOUS BATTLES

Nobunaga's military genius is best demonstrated in two of his most famous battles: the Battle of Okehazama in 1560 and the Battle of Nagashino in 1575. These battles showcase his ability to employ unconventional tactics and leverage new technologies to overcome seemingly insurmountable odds.

BATTLE OF OKEHAZAMA (桶狭間の戦い, 1560)

The Battle of Okehazama was one of the defining moments in Nobunaga's early military career. Facing an invading force from Imagawa Yoshimoto (今川 義元) that was estimated to outnumber his own troops tenfold, Nobunaga orchestrated a daring and decisive surprise attack. As Imagawa's forces were celebrating what they believed to be an imminent victory, Nobunaga led a small, elite force to attack the camp, catching the enemy completely off guard. The result was a stunning victory for Nobunaga, who personally led the charge and killed Imagawa Yoshimoto, causing his forces to flee in panic.[41]

---

[41] Varley, P. (2005). Warfare in Japan 1467–1600. In *War in the early modern world* (pp. 53-86). Routledge.

BATTLE OF NAGASHINO (長篠の戦い, 1575)

At the Battle of Nagashino, Nobunaga's innovative use of firearms reached its peak. Facing the Takeda clan, known for their powerful cavalry, Nobunaga devised a strategy that would neutralize the Takeda cavalry charges. He constructed wooden palisades and deployed 3,000 arquebusiers behind these defenses, where they could fire in succession, cutting down the advancing cavalry before they could reach his lines. The result was a devastating defeat for the Takeda forces, with most of their cavalry destroyed, marking the beginning of the end for the Takeda clan.

According to Turnbull (2003) in *Samurai: The World of the Warrior*, Nobunaga's volley fire was a decisive factor:

"Nobunaga's innovative use of arquebuses in volley fire, combined with the defensive palisades, utterly devastated the Takeda cavalry, making the battle one of the most significant turning points in Sengoku warfare."

CRUELTY AND MASSACRES

While Nobunaga's military prowess was widely acknowledged, his ruthlessness and cruelty have made him a highly controversial figure in Japanese history. His brutal suppression of enemies, especially those who opposed him on religious grounds, has left a lasting legacy of fear and admiration.

SIEGE OF MOUNT HIEI (比叡山焼き討ち, 1571)

One of the most infamous acts of Nobunaga's rule was the destruction of the Enryaku-ji temple complex on Mount Hiei in 1571. Enryaku-ji, home to the Tendai Buddhist sect, had long been a center of political and military resistance to Nobunaga's ambitions. Frustrated by the monks' resistance and their ability to mobilize warriors (僧兵, sōhei), Nobunaga ordered the complete destruction of the temple complex, resulting in the massacre of thousands of monks, women, and children.

Sansom in *A History of Japan* describes this as one of the most brutal events of Nobunaga's career:

"The wholesale slaughter at Enryaku-ji, where Nobunaga's forces burned the temple and massacred all within, including women and children, remains one of the darkest stains on his career, illustrating his ruthless determination to annihilate any opposition."[42]

---

[42] Sansom, George (1961). *A History of Japan, 1334–1615*. Stanford University Press.

NAGASHIMA MASSACRE (長島一向一揆, 1574)

Similarly, Nobunaga's campaign against the Ikkō-ikki (一向一揆), a group of warrior monks and peasants who opposed his rule, was marked by extreme cruelty. The Ikkō-ikki had resisted Nobunaga's authority for years, and after several failed attempts to subdue them, Nobunaga decided to destroy their stronghold at Nagashima. In 1574, he ordered the complete destruction of Nagashima, burning it to the ground and killing tens of thousands of Ikkō-ikki, including civilians.

Varley in *Japanese Culture* explains that Nobunaga's determination to eliminate any source of rebellion was both strategic and personal:

"Nobunaga's treatment of the Ikkō-ikki was not just a political necessity but a personal vendetta against those who dared to challenge his authority. His brutality at Nagashima was a clear message to all who resisted him."[43]

---

[43] Varley, P. (2000). *Japanese Culture: Fourth Edition.* University of Hawai'i Press. http://www.jstor.org/stable/j.ctt6wqxxp

PERSONAL LIFE AND SEXUALITY

Nobunaga's deep bond with certain young men, especially Mori Ranmaru (森 蘭丸),[44] has led many historians to question the nature of his relationships, exploring whether they were purely based on loyalty and duty, or if they extended into the realm of romantic and sexual intercourse. To fully understand Nobunaga's relationships with men, we must first place them within the context of samurai culture of the time, where such relationships were often structured under the accepted practice of shudō (衆道).

RELATIONSHIPS WITH MEN: NOBUNAGA AND MORI RANMARU

One of the most talked-about figures in Nobunaga's inner circle was Mori Ranmaru, a young and exceptionally beautiful retainer who served as one of Nobunaga's most trusted bodyguards. The relationship between Nobunaga and Ranmaru has been romanticized over the centuries, particularly due to their tragic deaths together during the Honnō-ji Incident (本能寺の変, 1582). In that fateful moment, when Nobunaga was betrayed by Akechi Mitsuhide (明智光秀) and surrounded by his enemies, Ranmaru

---

[44] 日埜博司, & ヒノヒロシ. (2005). 『コリャード懺悔録』ポルトガル語全訳注: 第六誡「邪淫を犯すべからず」に関わる 15 の告解. *流通經濟大學論集*, *40*(1), 111-165.

remained by his side, choosing to die with his lord rather than flee. Ranmaru's loyalty was seen as absolute, and his sacrifice has been interpreted as a final testament to the deep bond between the two men.

Historical sources often highlight Ranmaru's beauty and youth, characteristics that were celebrated in the context of shudō, a practice that was common among the samurai class. Shudō refers to male-male relationships between adult samurai and younger apprentices, typically wakashū (若衆), boys in their teens. These relationships, while sometimes involving sexual activity, were also centered on emotional connection, mentorship, and loyalty and were not always sexual. These relationships disturbing as they may be when sexual, were not stigmatized in 16th-century Japan; rather, they were often seen as a way of fostering bonds between warriors.

The nature of Nobunaga's relationship with Ranmaru has long been a subject of debate among historians. Some, such as Ihara Saikaku, a 17th-century author who wrote extensively about shudō in works like *The Great Mirror of Male Love* (男色大鑑, Nanshoku Ōkagami)[45], celebrated the virtues of male-male samurai relationships. Modern scholars, have suggested that Nobunaga's

---

[45] Saikaku, Ihara. (1687). *The Great Mirror of Male Love* (男色大鑑, Nanshoku Ōkagami). [Translated into English by Paul Gordon Schalow].

relationships with his male retainers were likely framed within this accepted practice. Nobunaga's close connection with Ranmaru, as well as with other young men in his personal bodyguard unit, may very well have extended beyond professional loyalty into the realm of romantic attachment and sexual activity, though this was not necessarily seen as something unusual or controversial in the period. It has been suggested by some that this may also be one area in which Nobunaga found an interest in Yasuke however the evidence is not conclusive and remains at best, speculation. So, it cannot be claimed that this was the case since it would be dishonest to do so.

DAIMYŌ AND SAMURAI HOMOSEXUALITY: THE CONTEXT OF SHUDŌ

To fully appreciate Nobunaga's potential relationships with men, it's essential to understand the broader cultural acceptance of shudō during the Sengoku period. The practice of shudō,[46] meaning "the way of the youths," involved relationships between adult men, often senior samurai or daimyō, and adolescent boys, typically aged between 12 and 18. If common folk were against the practice, it stands to reason that there would be little possibility of intervention as samurai were able to kill commoners if they felt offended, this concept of "right to cut down" (斬捨御免, *kirisute*

---

[46] Goldman, E. J. (2023). Tokugawa Era Conceptions of Samurai Honor.

gomen) was beginning to form during Sengoku (戦国時代) and would later be formalized into law during Edo period (江戸時代).[47]

In the world of the samurai, shudō was not seen as something that conflicted with a man's heterosexual obligations, such as marriage or fathering children. These relationships were often formative, as they trained the younger partner, usually a wakashū, in both military skill and the ethical codes of the samurai.[48]

Nobunaga's close relationships with young men, like Ranmaru, may well have been a reflection of this cultural practice. Surrounded by handsome and loyal retainers, many of whom were noted for their beauty and youth, Nobunaga fit the mold of a powerful samurai lord who engaged in shudō and highlights his potential interest in Yasuke, but despite claims from many there simply is no record of this being true.

---

[47] Bodart-Bailey, B. M. (2006). *The dog shogun: the personality and policies of Tokugawa Tsunayoshi*. University of Hawaii Press.

[48] Leupp, G. (2023). *Male colors: The construction of homosexuality in Tokugawa Japan*. Univ of California Press.

HETEROSEXUAL RELATIONSHIPS: NOBUNAGA AND NŌHIME

While much of the focus on Nobunaga's personal relationships centers on his male retainers, his heterosexual relationships also played a key role in his life. Nobunaga was married to Nōhime (濃姫), the daughter of Saitō Dōsan (斎藤道三), in a political marriage that helped to solidify the alliance between the Oda clan and the powerful Saitō clan of Mino Province (美濃国). This marriage, like many political unions during the Sengoku period, was less about romantic attachment and more about strategic consolidation of power. Nōhime, also known as Lady Kichō (帰蝶), played an important role in maintaining the alliance between the two clans, though little is recorded about the emotional or personal dynamics of their relationship.

Nobunaga did father children, most notably Oda Nobutada (織田信忠), his heir and eventual successor, as well as several other sons who held various military and political positions. However, unlike his relationship with Ranmaru, Nobunaga's romantic life with women is not as widely documented. It's important to note that, during this time, marriage and romantic relationships were often distinct from each other, with marriages serving political purposes while more personal, romantic relationships might be found elsewhere.

CRUELTY TOWARDS THE POPULATION AND HIS BRUTAL RULE

Oda Nobunaga's rise to power was not only marked by his military genius but also by his extreme unforgiving nature toward those who opposed him. He had little tolerance for disloyalty, rebellion, or dissent. Whether dealing with rival daimyō (大名), religious sects, or civilian uprisings, Nobunaga's responses were often characterized by brutality. His actions were not just meant to defeat opponents but to send a message to others that resistance would be met with severe and often deadly consequences.

UNFORGIVING TOWARD DISSENT

Far from being a liberator of the people, Nobunaga's strategy in dealing with rivals or anyone who posed a threat to his authority was one of total annihilation. His approach to warfare and governance was ruthless; he left no room for negotiation with those who defied him. Once someone rebelled or showed signs of disloyalty, Nobunaga would often respond with swift and brutal force.

For example, Nobunaga's elimination of his younger brother, Oda Nobuyuki (織田信行), is a testament to his hardline stance. Nobuyuki had conspired against Nobunaga, and though Nobunaga initially forgave him, after a second conspiracy attempt, Nobuyuki was executed. Nobunaga's method of dealing with dissent was uncompromising, ensuring that his own family, let alone outsiders, would not challenge his rule without dire consequences.

DESTRUCTION OF TEMPLES AND SHRINES

One of Nobunaga's most infamous campaigns was his assault on Buddhist sects, particularly his long-standing conflict with the Ikkō-ikki (一向一揆), a group of warrior monks and peasants who had banded together in a form of religious and social rebellion. The Ikkō-ikki controlled fortified temples and were staunch opponents of Nobunaga's growing power, presenting a unique challenge as they combined religious zeal with military force.

Nobunaga's response to the Ikkō-ikki was unrelenting. His siege of Nagashima (長島一向一揆, 1574), where thousands of Ikkō-ikki members were slaughtered and their stronghold was burned to the ground,[49] is a grim example of his willingness to use total warfare against those who resisted him. The culmination of his anti-Buddhist campaigns, however, was the destruction of Enryaku-ji (延暦寺) on Mount Hiei (比叡山) in 1571.

---

[49] Turnbull, S. (2012). *Nagashino 1575: Slaughter at the barricades* (Vol. 69). Bloomsbury Publishing.

Enryaku-ji, a sprawling temple complex that served as the headquarters for the Tendai sect (天台宗) of Buddhism, had long been a thorn in Nobunaga's side. The monks of Mount Hiei were powerful and often involved themselves in political matters, aligning themselves with Nobunaga's enemies. Frustrated by their resistance, Nobunaga ordered a total assault on the temple. His forces burned Enryaku-ji to the ground, killing not only the warrior monks but also thousands of non-combatants, including women and children. This massacre remains one of the most notorious and brutal events in Japanese history.

The destruction of Enryaku-ji was not just a strategic move to eliminate a powerful religious and military force; it was also meant to send a clear message to anyone who dared oppose Nobunaga. By eradicating a sacred religious site and slaughtering all within, Nobunaga demonstrated his willingness to go to any lengths to secure his power.

DEHUMANIZING HIS ENEMIES

Nobunaga's treatment of his enemies often went beyond mere military defeat. He regularly subjected them to humiliation and torture before death. Publicly humiliating his enemies was a deliberate tactic to undermine their status and to show his own dominance. His practice of making examples of rebels—whether rival daimyō, religious leaders, or common people—was meant to instill fear across the population.

Entire populations were sometimes wiped out if they were deemed to be too rebellious or problematic. Nobunaga's destruction of the Asakura clan (朝倉氏) and the Azai clan (浅井氏) are examples of his preference for total annihilation over diplomacy.[50] Both clans, initially allies, later opposed Nobunaga. In his campaigns against them, Nobunaga not only decimated their armies but also slaughtered large portions of their populations, ensuring that no remnants of their resistance could re-emerge.

Nobunaga's cruelty extended to the treatment of captured enemies. It was common for him to execute prisoners in painful and public ways, using torture as a method of control and terror. These public displays were calculated acts meant to demonstrate the consequences of rebellion. Nobunaga's deliberate use of brutality helped solidify his fearsome reputation and deter future resistance.

PUBLIC EXECUTIONS

Public executions were a key part of Nobunaga's rule. His use of violence as a spectacle ensured that his enemies understood the consequences of opposing him, while also reinforcing his authority

---

[50] Streich, P. (2009). The Failure of the Balance of Power in Medieval Japan, 1568-1600. In *APSA 2009 Toronto Meeting Paper*.

to those under his control. Public executions of rival leaders or rebellious peasants served as a warning, making it clear that defiance would lead to death, often in a gruesome and highly visible manner.

One of the most significant public executions carried out under Nobunaga's orders was that of Azai Nagamasa (浅井 長政), his former brother-in-law. Nagamasa had initially allied with Nobunaga through marriage but later turned against him. After the fall of Odani Castle (小谷城), Nagamasa was captured and beheaded. Nobunaga displayed Nagamasa's head publicly, along with the heads of his other enemies, as a brutal reminder of what happened to those who opposed him. In many cases, the heads of captured enemies would be placed on display for several days to serve as a warning to others.[51]

In addition to beheadings, Nobunaga would also use other forms of execution, such as crucifixion and burning at the stake, especially for enemies who had committed acts of betrayal or rebellion. These public executions were designed to be as humiliating and dehumanizing as possible, reinforcing the idea that those who rebelled against Nobunaga would not only lose their lives but also their dignity.

---

[51] Ōta, G. (2011). *The Chronicle of Lord Nobunaga* (Vol. 36). Brill.

DEVELOPMENT OF SAMURAI SYSTEM

The claim that the samurai system was not fully developed during Yasuke's time is historically inaccurate. By the time Yasuke arrived in Japan in 1579, the samurai class was already well-established and had played a central role in Japan's political and military landscape for centuries.

THE SEMANTICS OF THE WORD "SAMURAI" (侍)

The word "samurai" (侍) comes from the verb "saburau" (侍う), which means "to serve" or "to attend to" someone of higher status. The kanji 侍 itself contains two components:

"人" (nin): The radical meaning "person."

"寺" (tera): This means "temple" or "monastery" but in this context serves as a phonetic component.

The semantics of 侍 suggest a person who serves or attends a lord, fitting their role in the Japanese feudal system. Samurai were expected to serve their daimyō (大名) loyally, following strict ethical codes that would later be formalized into Bushidō (武士道, the "Way of the Warrior").

EARLY HISTORICAL MENTIONS OF SAMURAI

The samurai system began to take form during the Heian period (平安時代) (794–1185 CE). While the warrior class didn't rise to full prominence until later, the early roots of the samurai can be traced back much earlier. Some of the first mentions of warrior groups and their role in society come from ancient Japanese literature.

EARLIEST MENTIONS IN JAPANESE LITERATURE

"Kojiki" (古事記, Record of Ancient Matters, 712 CE): This is one of Japan's oldest chronicles, and while it doesn't explicitly use the term "samurai," it refers to warrior figures and military exploits. These early warriors are the predecessors of what would later be known as samurai.

"Nihon Shoki" (日本書紀, Chronicles of Japan, 720 CE): Another early text, which, like the Kojiki, recounts the deeds of early Japanese warriors. The text discusses the military activities of the aristocracy, which helped lay the foundation for the future samurai class.

"Konjaku Monogatari" (今昔物語, Tales of Times Now Past, late Heian period): This collection of stories contains accounts of warriors, bandits, and military skirmishes, reflecting the growing importance of military figures in the Heian period. These stories show the transition of noble warriors into what would become the samurai class.

"Heike Monogatari" (平家物語, Tale of the Heike, early 13th century): This epic chronicles the Genpei War (源平合戦, 1180–1185), a conflict between the Taira and Minamoto clans that ultimately led to the rise of the samurai class. The Genpei War marks the end of the Heian period and the beginning of the Kamakura period (鎌倉時代, 1185–1333), when the samurai would become the dominant force in Japan.

THE ESTABLISHMENT OF THE SAMURAI SYSTEM

The Kamakura period (鎌倉時代) saw the establishment of the first shogunate, led by Minamoto no Yoritomo (源頼朝). During this time, the warrior class, or samurai, began to solidify its role as the governing military elite. The system of military rule under the samurai developed into a rigid hierarchical structure, where loyalty to one's lord and military prowess were paramount. This system would continue to evolve but was fully in place well before Yasuke's time.

By the Sengoku period (戦国時代) (1467–1615), the samurai were not only the dominant military force but also key political players. Powerful daimyōs like Oda Nobunaga (織田信長), Toyotomi Hideyoshi (豊臣秀吉), and later Tokugawa Ieyasu (徳川家康) were all samurai who shaped the course of Japanese history.

The formalization of the samurai class as a noble warrior caste in Japan underwent significant development over several historical periods, beginning in the Heian period (平安時代) and reaching a high degree of structure by the Edo period (江戸時代). Below is an overview of how each period contributed to the establishment and refinement of the samurai class.

HEIAN PERIOD (平安時代) (794–1185 CE)

Origin of the Samurai: The Heian period saw the early formation of the samurai as a distinct military class. Originally, the emperor's government relied on a system of conscription to maintain military forces. However, over time, wealthy landowners (豪族, gōzoku) began to hire private warriors to protect their estates from bandits and rival clans. These warriors, later known as samurai (侍),

initially served as mounted archers and were not yet part of a formal, noble class.[52][53]

Early Usage of the Term Samurai: The term "samurai" was first used in its rudimentary form during this period, derived from the verb 侍る (saburau), meaning "to serve" or "to attend." It referred to the warriors who served the imperial court and aristocrats. Early references to warriors in this role can be found in classical literature such as "The Tale of the Heike" (平家物語), though the samurai at this time had not yet fully developed into a formal caste.

Proto-Samurai: Although samurai did not yet represent a fully formalized caste, the roots of their identity as professional soldiers bound by loyalty to landowning aristocrats were firmly established in this era. Clan warfare became more frequent, and the samurai's skills in mounted combat, archery, and loyalty to their masters set them apart as a specialized group.

---

[52] 今昔物語集(Konjaku Monogatari-shū), "Tales of Times Now Past" (circa. 1120 and 1140 CE)by Minamoto no Takakuni (源 隆国)

[53] 平家物語 (Heike Monogatari, Tale of the Heike) circa 1219–1240 CE. Some of the most well-known written versions were compiled during the Kamakura period (鎌倉時代), including the *Kakuichi-bon* (覚一本), which was transcribed by the blind monk Kakuichi (覚一) around 1371 CE.

KAMAKURA PERIOD (鎌倉時代) (1185–1333 CE)

The Rise of the Samurai as Ruling Class: The Kamakura period marked a critical turning point in the formalization of the samurai class. After the Genpei War (源平合戦), which ended in 1185 with the establishment of the Kamakura shogunate (鎌倉幕府), the samurai, under the leadership of the Minamoto clan (源氏), became the de facto rulers of Japan. The emperor retained a symbolic role, but real power lay with the shogun (将軍), the military leader supported by samurai. [54],[55]

Samurai as Landholders: During this period, samurai were rewarded with land (知行地, chigyōchi) for their military service, solidifying their status as a hereditary warrior class. The hierarchical system of vassalage (主従関係, shujū kankei) was formalized, where lower-ranking samurai pledged loyalty to higher-ranking daimyō (大名), creating a structured feudal system.

Bushidō Origins: The code of bushidō (武士道), the "way of the warrior," began to take shape during this period, emphasizing virtues such as loyalty, honor, and martial skill. Although bushidō

---

[54] 方丈記 (Hōjōki) (1212).

[55] 吾妻鏡(Azuma Kagami "Mirror of the East")(Circa. 1266)

was not fully codified at this point, the warrior ethos that defined the samurai started to emerge.

MUROMACHI PERIOD (室町時代) (1336–1573 CE)

Further Refinement of Samurai Power: The Muromachi period saw the consolidation of samurai power through the Ashikaga shogunate (足利幕府). The samurai class became more politically influential, with many samurai families holding large territories and exercising authority over both military and civil matters.[56]

Cultural Flourishing and Samurai Patronage: Samurai during this period were not only warriors but also patrons of the arts, and their role expanded beyond the battlefield. Tea ceremonies (茶道), Noh theater (能), and ink painting flourished under samurai sponsorship, contributing to the cultural prestige of the class.[57]

The Samurai as Noble Warriors: By the end of the Muromachi period, samurai were firmly entrenched as a noble warrior caste. They were distinguished not only by their martial skills but also by their role as regional administrators and their participation in the cultural life of the nation.[58]

---

[56] 太平記 (Taiheiki) (1371)

[57] 金海和歌集 (Kinkai Wakashū) 1403

[58] 義経記 (Gikeiki) (Circa.1371–1372)

SENGOKU PERIOD (戦国時代) (1467–1600 CE)

Warring States and Increased Militarization: The Sengoku period, or Warring States period, saw the rise of powerful daimyō who controlled vast territories and their own private armies of samurai.[59] The constant warfare during this era led to the further militarization of the samurai class, with a strong focus on battlefield tactics, leadership, and loyalty.[60]

Elevation of Peasant-Samurai: Social mobility allowed skilled individuals from non-samurai backgrounds to rise through the ranks and become samurai, especially through successful military service. This period saw the emergence of a new class of foot soldiers (足軽, ashigaru), who could be promoted into the samurai class based on merit and battlefield success over a period of many years.[61]

Samurai Ethics in Warfare: During the Sengoku period, the principles of loyalty and honor became central to samurai life, particularly in the context of their relationships with their lords (君

---

[59] 竹馬抄 (Chikubashō) (1548) by Imagawa Ryōshun (今川了俊)
[60] 甲冑記 (Katchūki) (Circa 1569–1610) possibly by Ōta Gyūichi (太田牛一)
[61] 北条五代記 (Hōjō Godaiki) (Circa. 1600)

主, kunshu). This period cemented many of the values that would later be codified into bushidō.

EDO PERIOD (江戸時代) (1603–1868 CE)

Formalization and Codification: The Edo period, under the Tokugawa shogunate (徳川幕府), saw the final formalization of the samurai class. The samurai were now a distinct, hereditary class above commoners and below the nobility. This period marked the strictest division of Japan's class system, with samurai having the exclusive right to bear arms.

Bureaucratization of Samurai: With the peace established under Tokugawa rule, many samurai took on bureaucratic and administrative roles, rather than serving primarily as warriors. Despite this shift away from constant military activity, the samurai retained their high social status and continued to uphold the ideals of loyalty and service.

Bushidō Codification: During this period, the ideals of bushidō were codified into formal doctrine. The Hagakure (葉隠), written by Yamamoto Tsunetomo, and other texts from the Edo period articulated the samurai code of conduct, which emphasized honor, loyalty, and the duty to one's lord, even in peacetime.

The Samurai as Cultural Guardians: Samurai also became the guardians of Japanese culture, literature, and education during the Edo period. They were expected to be well-versed in the arts, Confucian teachings, and Zen philosophy, reflecting their role as both warriors and scholars.

During the Sengoku period (戦国時代, 1467–1603), Japan's social hierarchy was complex and rigid, though it was marked by more social mobility due to the chaotic nature of the era. The breakdown of social classes, from the lowest to the highest, is as follows:

SLAVES (奴隷, DOREI)

Status: The lowest class in Sengoku society.

Description: Slaves were typically prisoners of war, criminals, or debtors who were forced into servitude. Slavery in Japan was not as widespread as in other parts of the world, but it existed in some form, particularly as part of warfare, where captured enemies were sometimes enslaved.

Role: They performed menial labor, such as working on farms or in the households of daimyō (大名, feudal lords) or samurai.

HININ (非人, "NON-PERSONS") AND ETA (穢多, "POLLUTED ONES")

Status: Outcasts or "untouchables."

Description: These people were outside the regular social order and were often engaged in work considered impure or polluting, such as animal slaughter, tanning hides, or handling the dead. The hinin also included beggars and criminals. Eta communities were segregated and heavily discriminated against.

Role: They performed jobs that others in society refused to do, including butchery, executioner roles, and leatherworking.

PEASANTS (農民, NŌMIN)

Status: The majority of the population.

Description: Peasants were farmers and laborers who worked the land, which was usually owned by the daimyō or the local samurai. They were heavily taxed and often exploited, but they were essential for producing the rice and crops that sustained the economy.

Role: Farming was their primary occupation, but they also performed other forms of manual labor. Peasants were tied to the land and could not easily move or change professions without the permission of their lords.

ARTISANS (職人, SHOKUNIN)

Status: Above peasants but below merchants in terms of prestige.

Description: Artisans were skilled craftsmen who made goods such as swords, pottery, and other items necessary for daily life or warfare. Although they were respected for their craft, they were considered less vital than farmers in this agrarian society.

Role: They produced tools, weapons, clothing, and various art objects. Their economic power was limited compared to the warrior class.

MERCHANTS (商人, SHŌNIN)

Status: Relatively low in status but could accumulate great wealth.

Description: Despite their wealth, merchants were seen as parasitic because they did not produce goods themselves but profited from the trade of goods. Their status was officially below peasants and artisans, although in reality, many became quite powerful due to their economic influence.

Role: Merchants traded goods, including rice, weapons, and other essential commodities. Some became extremely wealthy, especially in major cities such as Sakai (堺) and Kyoto (京都), and would sponsor samurai or temples to gain protection or status.

SAMURAI (侍) AND ASHIGARU (足軽, FOOT SOLDIERS)

Samurai (侍):

Status: The warrior class and holders of power.

Description: The samurai were the ruling class during the Sengoku period. They were not only warriors but also administrators, overseeing lands and governing local populations. They were vassals to the daimyō and bound by the code of honor known as bushidō (武士道).

Role: Samurai provided military service to their daimyō and were expected to demonstrate loyalty, bravery, and martial skill. In exchange, they were granted land or stipends and had authority over the peasants.

Ashigaru (足軽):

Status: Low-ranking soldiers, often considered the "foot soldiers" of the samurai armies.

Description: The ashigaru were commoners who took up arms, often recruited during times of war. Though of lower status than full samurai, successful ashigaru could rise in rank through bravery and martial prowess.

Role: They served as the backbone of the daimyō's armies, performing essential tasks such as garrisoning, fighting, and protecting the lands.

DAIMYŌ (大名, FEUDAL LORDS)

Status: Powerful regional lords.

Description: The daimyō were the highest-ranking members of the warrior class and ruled large territories. They were often in conflict with one another during the Sengoku period, each striving to increase their land and power. They governed vast stretches of land and had their own armies, often engaging in warfare to consolidate power.

Role: The daimyō were responsible for maintaining order, collecting taxes, administering justice, and raising armies to protect and expand their territories.

SHŌGUN (将軍, MILITARY DICTATOR)

Status: The highest-ranking military leader.

Description: The shōgun was the de facto ruler of Japan, with the emperor acting as a figurehead. By the Sengoku period, the

Ashikaga shogunate (足利幕府) had weakened, leading to the rise of powerful daimyōs, but the concept of shōgunate authority remained important.

Role: The shōgun was responsible for maintaining military control over Japan and overseeing the daimyō. However, during the Sengoku period, the Ashikaga shogunate had lost much of its power, and the authority of the shōgun was often challenged by the daimyōs.

EMPEROR (天皇, TENNŌ)

Status: The nominal head of Japan, but with little real political power during the Sengoku period.

Description: The emperor was the ceremonial and spiritual leader of Japan, believed to be descended from the gods (kami), but during the Sengoku period, his influence was mostly symbolic. Real power lay with the shōgun and the daimyōs.

Role: The emperor performed important religious and cultural functions, such as conferring titles or divine legitimacy on rulers, but did not engage in the governance of the country.

SOCIAL MOBILITY IN THE SENGOKU PERIOD:

While the social structure was rigid, the constant warfare of the Sengoku period allowed for some mobility, especially within the samurai class. Ashigaru, for example, could rise to the rank of samurai through exceptional service, and some peasants could improve their standing by serving daimyōs or participating in warfare. This era was one of the few in Japanese history where such upward mobility was possible due to the unsettled political landscape but that was nonetheless rare.[62]

---

[62] Park, D. (2013). *A vehicle of social mobility: Utilitarian factors in the rise of Neo-Confucianism in the early Tokugawa period.* University of Illinois at Urbana-Champaign.

BUSHIDO- WAY OF THE SAMURAI

The European knight system and the Japanese samurai system are often compared because both represent the warrior aristocracy of their respective societies. While they share certain similarities, such as their focus on honor, military service, and feudal loyalty, the cultural, philosophical, and social contexts of these two warrior classes are vastly different. Western audiences sometimes confuse the two, often perceiving knights and samurai as equivalent figures. However, a closer examination reveals significant differences in their roles, codes of conduct, training, and their positions in their respective societies.

FEUDAL STRUCTURES AND ROLES

Both knights in medieval Europe and samurai (侍) in feudal Japan were integral parts of the feudal system, serving lords (daimyō in Japan and lords or kings in Europe) in exchange for land or privileges. However, the feudal systems in which they operated were quite different in structure and function.

European Knights: The European knight system was based on a rigid feudal hierarchy where knights served as vassals to a lord or king, often receiving fiefs (land) in return for their military service. The relationship between a knight and his lord was formalized through homage and fealty, with knights pledging military service and loyalty in exchange for protection and land to govern. Knights often oversaw their own manors and were responsible for maintaining local law and order, in addition to serving as elite soldiers.

Japanese Samurai: The samurai system was also feudal but developed quite differently. Samurai served their daimyō (大名) or the shogun (将軍), not always in exchange for land but often in the form of stipends, paid in rice. Unlike European knights, who were often landowners, samurai were more closely tied to a bureaucratic military hierarchy and were deeply embedded in the political structure of their domain. Samurai were expected to be loyal not just to their immediate lord but also to a broader code of ethics, known as bushidō (武士道), which dictated their behavior both on and off the battlefield.

CODES OF CONDUCT: CHIVALRY VS. BUSHIDŌ

The moral and ethical frameworks governing knights and samurai—chivalry and bushidō—are often compared, but they emerged from very different cultural and religious contexts.

Chivalry (European Knights): The code of chivalry was influenced by Christian values and revolved around concepts of honor, bravery, loyalty, and courtly love. Knights were expected to protect the weak, defend the church, and remain loyal to their lords.[63] The chivalric code, while idealized in literature, was not always consistently practiced and was more flexible depending on the political and military situation. Over time, chivalry also came to include aspects of romantic love, with knights serving as protectors of noble women, sometimes leading to the concept of "courtly love."

Bushidō (Samurai): The samurai code, bushidō, was heavily influenced by Zen Buddhism, Confucianism, and Shinto beliefs. Bushidō emphasized honor, loyalty, self-discipline, and duty to one's lord, often to the point of death. Unlike the Christian undertones of chivalry, bushidō's values were tied to the philosophical and spiritual beliefs of impermanence and self-sacrifice. One key difference is the concept of seppuku (切腹)[64], or ritual suicide, which was viewed as an honorable way to restore

---

[63] Keen, M. (2020). Chivalry. In *Gentry culture in late-medieval England* (pp. 35-49). Manchester University Press.

[64] Ikegami, E. (2003). Shame and the samurai: Institutions, trusthworthiness, and autonomy in the elite honor culture. *Social Research: An International Quarterly, 70*(4), 1351-1378.

one's honor or demonstrate loyalty, a practice entirely absent in the European knightly system.

MILITARY TRAINING AND WARFARE

Both knights and samurai were elite warriors, but their training, equipment, and roles in warfare were influenced by the environments and cultures they were raised in.

European Knights: Knights were heavy cavalry, heavily armored and trained to fight on horseback with weapons like lances, swords, and maces. Their primary role in battle was as shock troops, charging into enemy formations to break their lines. The development of knights was largely influenced by the agricultural economy of Europe, which provided the resources necessary to equip a heavily armored horseman. The use of fortified castles and siege warfare was central to knightly battles, and knights often had a defensive role as well, overseeing fortifications.

Samurai: Samurai were primarily mounted archers in the early stages of their history, but they also engaged in swordsmanship and close-quarters combat. Samurai relied on a range of weapons, including the katana (刀), yari (槍, spear), naginta (長刀, pole weapon), and bow (弓). Samurai armor, such as the ō-yoroi (大鎧), was designed for greater mobility compared to the full plate armor of European knights. Over time, as firearms were introduced to

Japan in the 16th century, samurai tactics adapted to include the use of arquebuses. Samurai were highly trained in the art of war, but their role was not just limited to warfare—they were also expected to be cultured individuals, knowledgeable in the arts, poetry, and calligraphy.

SOCIAL AND CULTURAL PERCEPTIONS

The social roles of knights and samurai were deeply integrated into their respective societies, but the cultural expectations placed on them were different.

European Knights: Knights were part of the nobility, but their role was often more militaristic and focused on feudal governance. The courtly love tradition in Europe meant that knights were often depicted as defenders of ladies and courtly virtue, roles that played a significant part in medieval European literature, such as the Arthurian legends. Knights were expected to uphold Christian values and were involved in crusades or religious warfare.

Samurai: Samurai were not only warriors but also administrators and scholars. In times of peace, samurai were expected to be cultured, practicing arts like tea ceremony (茶道), poetry (和歌), and painting. The ideal of the warrior-poet was important in samurai culture. Samurai were often portrayed as embodying the highest ideals of stoicism and loyalty, and their lives were meant to reflect the philosophical tenets of self-discipline and honor, even in non-military contexts.

CONFUSION AND MISCONCEPTIONS

The confusion between the two systems often arises in Western popular culture, where samurai are sometimes portrayed as the "Japanese equivalent" of knights. This perception likely stems from their shared role as elite warriors bound by a code of conduct, serving a feudal lord. However, this comparison overlooks the deep cultural, philosophical, and religious differences that shaped their distinct identities.

While both knights and samurai served as the military elite of their societies, the knight's identity was closely tied to Christian values and feudal governance, whereas the samurai were deeply influenced by Buddhist, Confucian, and Shinto ideals, which emphasized self-discipline, honor in death, and cultural refinement in times of peace.

The process of becoming a samurai (侍) in feudal Japan was a long and demanding journey, starting in childhood and requiring rigorous training, discipline, and adherence to the ethical code of bushidō (武士道). This path was deeply ingrained in the samurai's class system, where children of samurai families were trained from an early age to uphold their family's honor and become warriors capable of serving their daimyō (大名) or the shogun (将軍).

APPRENTICESHIP AS A WAKASHŪ (若衆)

A boy destined to become a samurai would typically begin his training as early as age 5 or 6. At this young age, he was referred to as a wakashū (若衆), a boy in his adolescence who would begin learning the basics of samurai life. He was often taken under the wing of an experienced samurai or a senior member of his family. This mentor would teach the boy about the virtues of bushidō, including loyalty (忠義, chūgi), courage (勇気, yūki), honor (名誉, meiyo), and self-discipline.

The wakashū would be trained both in physical skills and in the development of mental and moral qualities. Training at this stage was basic and focused on obedience, respect for elders, and discipline. The young boy would also begin learning etiquette (礼儀, *reigi*) and the proper behavior expected of a samurai, particularly in social settings.

TRAINING IN THE MARTIAL ARTS (武芸, BUGEI)

As the boy grew older, usually around age 10 or 12, he would begin serious training in the martial arts, known as bugei (武芸).

The martial disciplines were diverse, but most samurai apprentices focused on mastering key weapons:

- Kenjutsu (剣術): Swordsmanship was one of the most important skills for a samurai, and kenjutsu, the art of the sword, was central to his training. The boy would first train with a bokken (木剣, wooden sword) before advancing to practice with real blades like the katana (刀) and the wakizashi (脇差).

- Kyūjutsu (弓術): Archery was a crucial skill for early samurai, especially in the Heian and Kamakura periods. The boy would train in the use of the yumi (弓, bow), learning how to shoot accurately from both foot and horseback.

- Bajutsu (馬術): Horsemanship was another key aspect of samurai training. The young samurai would learn how to ride horses in battle, practicing mounted combat with both the bow and the sword.

- Sōjutsu (槍術): Spear training, or sōjutsu, involved learning to use the yari (槍, spear), a primary weapon in many battlefield engagements. Samurai were expected to master multiple weapons, and proficiency with the spear was a fundamental part of their education.

At this stage, physical training would also include grappling and hand-to-hand combat, such as jujutsu (柔術), and the boy would be taught the importance of flexibility and adaptability in combat situations. Physical endurance training, long hours of practice, and sparring with peers were all part of the rigorous daily routine.

STUDY OF PHILOSOPHY AND LITERATURE

In addition to his martial training, a young samurai would also receive a well-rounded education in literature and philosophy. Samurai were expected to be as cultured as they were skilled in warfare, following the ideal of the warrior-scholar. Samurai boys would study classical Chinese texts, particularly those by Confucius, whose teachings on loyalty, duty, and morality heavily influenced bushidō.

Calligraphy (書道, shodō) and poetry (和歌, waka) were considered essential arts for a samurai. Calligraphy, for example, was not merely a means of communication but an expression of discipline, self-control, and aesthetic sensibility. A boy's education in bushidō emphasized the balance between martial prowess and the refinement of one's mind and character.

Zen Buddhism was also a key philosophical influence on samurai training. The principles of meditation (zazen, 座禅) and mindfulness in battle, as well as the acceptance of impermanence and death, shaped the psychological aspect of samurai warfare. By confronting the concept of mortality head-on, a samurai was taught to embrace selflessness and to face battle without fear.

RANKS FROM KOSHŌ (小姓) TO SAMURAI

The path to becoming a fully recognized samurai (侍) was a gradual and demanding process that began with lower ranks and stages of development. A young boy, often from a samurai family or one chosen for service, would move through these ranks, each reflecting the military structure and social hierarchy of samurai life during the Azuchi-Momoyama period (安土桃山時代, 1573–1600). The following outlines the main ranks on the journey from a young servant to a fully recognized samurai.

SWORD-BEARER/ ASSISTANT-RETAINER (KOSHŌ 小姓)

The first and lowest rank was koshō, which referred to a personal attendant or page in the service of a samurai or daimyō (大名). Boys selected for this role were typically from samurai families, though some came from lower ranks and some remained in this role for a lifetime as a sort of personal assistant. Their duties primarily involved:

- Carrying their master's sword or armor during travel or public events.

- Assisting with personal tasks, such as helping their master dress in formal attire or armor.
- Acting as messengers, relaying instructions and information between their master and other retainers.[65]
- Observing the lifestyle, manners, and strategy of their masters, learning etiquette and discipline while gaining insight into the warrior's life.

Although the role of koshō involved personal service, it was a training ground for young boys who would eventually potentially advance to higher ranks. A koshō was not yet a warrior, but his close proximity to powerful samurai allowed him to learn valuable lessons in loyalty, protocol, and combat preparation.

RETAINER (従者, JŪSHA)

As the boy matured, he would be promoted to the rank of retainer (従者, jūsha), where his responsibilities expanded beyond simple attendance to his master. Retainers were often apprentices who assisted more experienced samurai or daimyō. Their tasks were still largely supportive, including:

---

[65] 江戸楽, & 編集部. (2022). *手紙が語る歴史秘話 書簡と現代語訳で日本史の裏側を読み解く~ 戦国武将から明治の文人まで~*. メイツ出版.

- Preparing armor and weapons for battle.

- Carrying weapons or other essential items for their master.

- Ensuring their master's comfort during travel or in the lord's household.

- Observing military tactics and participating in the logistics of their lord's campaigns.

Although retainers were considered part of the warrior class, they were still in a subordinate position and not yet regarded as full warriors. Their role was focused on service and learning, with their actions constantly monitored by their masters.

FOOT SOLDIER (足軽, ASHIGARU)

Once the retainer gained sufficient experience, he might serve as an ashigaru (足軽, foot soldier). Ashigaru were the infantry troops of the warrior class, typically drawn from the lower ranks of samurai families or even commoners. The ashigaru were heavily involved in military campaigns during the Sengoku period (戦国時代) and the Azuchi-Momoyama period and made up the majority of soldiers in most armies.

As an ashigaru, the young samurai would receive training in combat and the use of various weapons, including:

- Spears (槍, yari).

- Bows (弓, yumi).
- Firearms, which had been introduced by the Portuguese in the mid-16th century.

Ashigaru were lightly armed and typically participated in the bulk of the fighting during battles. Although they did not have the privileged status of full samurai, their experience on the battlefield was essential for gaining the skills and knowledge needed to advance to higher ranks.

GENPUKU (元服)

The genpuku (元服) ceremony marked the young boy's transition from childhood to adulthood and into the samurai class. This ceremony was a significant milestone in a young samurai's life, representing the beginning of his formal training in martial arts and military responsibilities. During the genpuku ceremony, the boy would be given:

- A wakizashi (脇差, short sword) as a symbol of his readiness to enter the world of samurai.
- His first adult clothing, signifying his move into adulthood.
- An adult name, often reflecting part of his lord's name as a mark of loyalty.

Despite the formalities of genpuku, this stage did not make the individual a full samurai. He still had to prove himself through combat experience, loyalty, and service to his master. The genpuku ceremony was more of a starting point, and from this moment forward, the young warrior would have to earn recognition and respect within the hierarchy.

GENPUKU (元服) AND ITS MEANING

The genpuku ceremony, typically performed around the ages of 14 to 16 but sometimes as young as 10 years of age[66], signified that the young man had reached adulthood and was ready to assume greater responsibilities as a samurai-in-training. During this ceremony, the youth was presented with an adult name and adult clothing, including the traditional eboshi (烏帽子, court cap), and, importantly, his first real sword, often a wakizashi (脇差, short sword). This ceremony symbolized his entrance into the bushi (武士, warrior) class, but it did not yet mean he had attained full samurai status.

The genpuku was, essentially, a coming-of-age ritual, but the young man still had much to learn before he could be considered a seasoned samurai. This period following the genpuku involved

---

[66] Machiko, Ō. (2021). *In the Shelter of the Pine: A Memoir of Yanagisawa Yoshiyasu and Tokugawa Japan*. Columbia University Press.

intensive training, battlefield experience, and the gradual assumption of leadership and administrative roles.

TRAINING AND BATTLEFIELD EXPERIENCE

After genpuku, the young man was expected to continue his martial training, but now he would also begin to participate in actual combat. This stage of his life was critical, as battlefield experience was the ultimate test of a samurai's skill, courage, and loyalty. In these battles, the young warrior would likely serve under the guidance of more experienced warriors, possibly family members or trusted veterans, who would mentor him and provide practical training in combat strategy and tactics.

During this time, the young warriorwould further refine his skills in kenjutsu (剣術, swordsmanship), kyūjutsu (弓術, archery), and sōjutsu (槍術, spear fighting), but also begin to study hyōhō (兵法, military strategy) more deeply. These skills would not just be taught in isolated drills but in the context of real warfare, where the young warrior would learn to apply his skills under the pressures of life-and-death situations.

This period also involved proving one's loyalty (忠義, chūgi) and honor (名誉, meiyo) in battle. It was common for a young samurai to take orders directly from his daimyō and to demonstrate his commitment to the samurai code, bushidō (武士道), through bravery, self-discipline (修行, shugyō), and humility (謙虚, kenkyō).[67]

SERVICE TO A DAIMYŌ (大名)

The next step after genpuku would involve securing a position of service under a daimyō or other samurai lord. While the young man's family likely already had some affiliation with a local warlord, the youth himself would have to prove his worth through continued loyalty, service, and demonstration of martial prowess.

The period of feudal service included a range of duties, from guarding the lord's estate to serving as an attendant or even as a military commander in training. These roles prepared the samurai to understand the hierarchical structure of samurai society and learn how to lead and manage others in the future.

Samurai were also expected to engage in administrative duties during times of peace. This often involved land management, overseeing peasants, and ensuring that the territories of the lord were well-run. This side of samurai life emphasized the need for intellectual development, reinforcing the notion that the samurai

---

[67] 北条氏綱. (1590). 北条氏綱言行録. 吉川弘文館.

太田牛一. (1596). 信長公記. (1987). 新潮社.

had to be as competent in governance and bureaucracy as they were on the battlefield.[68]

SERVICE AND MASTERY: GIRI (義理) AND NINJO (人情)

After reaching adulthood, the samurai would continue his lifelong service to his daimyō or shogun, living according to the principles of giri (義理, duty) and ninjo (人情, human compassion). Giri, or duty, was central to the samurai's life and required absolute loyalty to his lord, family, and community. The samurai's duty was not only to protect and fight but also to uphold justice and serve as a model of ethical behavior.

A samurai was also bound by ninjo, the emotional and human aspect of life that had to be balanced with duty. This tension between personal emotions and societal expectations created many of the ethical dilemmas faced by samurai, particularly in periods of peace or internal conflict.

ADVANCED TRAINING AND LEADERSHIP

As a samurai matured and proved himself in battle, he would continue refining his martial skills and philosophical understanding. The study of strategy (兵法, hyōhō), as developed

---

[68] 大道寺友山. (1685). 武道初心集.

by famous samurai like Miyamoto Musashi (宮本武蔵)[69] and Yagyū Munenori (柳生宗矩), became a critical part of a senior samurai's training. Samurai would also be expected to serve in positions of leadership, overseeing the training of younger warriors or managing aspects of the lord's estate.

Samurai in positions of leadership would be responsible not just for their own conduct but for ensuring that the samurai code and military discipline were maintained throughout the ranks. The ability to lead, whether in combat or in administration, was a reflection of the samurai's dedication to his lifelong training and adherence to bushidō.

SAMURAI (侍)

Only after years of training, loyal service, and participation in battle would the young man be recognized as a full-fledged samurai. At this stage, the samurai would be expected to master a variety of martial arts, including:

- Kenjutsu (剣術, swordsmanship): Mastery of the katana (刀) and wakizashi.
- Kyūjutsu (弓術, archery): Proficiency with the bow and long-range combat.

---

[69] Musashi, M. (2016). *The Five Rings: Miyamoto Musashi's Art of Strategy*. Chartwell Books.

- Sōjutsu (槍術, spear-fighting): Expertise with the spear for close combat.
- Bajutsu (馬術, horsemanship): The ability to fight on horseback, which was vital for samurai warfare.

In addition to these martial skills, the full samurai would also take on social and military responsibilities. Many samurai served as retainers to a daimyō, helping manage land, collect taxes, and maintain order in their lord's domain. As a fully recognized samurai, one was expected to live by the strict code of bushidō (武士道), which emphasized honor (名誉, meiyo), loyalty (忠義, chūgi), self-discipline, and a willingness to lay down one's life in the service of their master.

It is important to note that in feudal Japan, becoming a samurai (侍) was not simply a matter of achieving martial skill or loyalty; it was deeply rooted in social status and heredity. The samurai class was tied to noble lineage, and the possession of a surname (姓, sei or 名字, myōji) was a key indicator of one's place within the bushi (武士) class. Having a surname signified that a person belonged to the warrior aristocracy or nobility, and it was an essential element of samurai identity.

BORN INTO A NOBLE FAMILY WITH A SURNAME

Most samurai were born into families that already held noble status and had a surname that connected them to the bushi class. These families had often served as retainers or warriors for generations, and their surnames were symbols of their hereditary rights and status within society. The possession of a surname indicated that the family had land, a position of service to a daimyō (大名), or other significant social roles within the feudal system. Samurai families often traced their lineage back to powerful clans (氏, uji) that had played important roles in Japanese history.

For example, major samurai clans like the Minamoto (源氏), Taira (平氏), and Fujiwara (藤原氏) were noble families with ancient surnames that signified their political and military importance. Being born into such a family meant that an individual was already part of the bushi class from birth, and their training as a samurai would begin early in life. In these cases, the surname was passed down through generations, symbolizing both the family's legacy and its commitment to samurai ideals.

GIFTED A SURNAME BY THE DAIMYŌ

However, not all samurai were born into noble families. In certain circumstances, a person who showed exceptional loyalty, martial skill, or service could be elevated to samurai status by their daimyō or samurai lord. When this happened, it was common for the daimyō to bestow upon the individual a surname, officially recognizing them as part of the samurai class.

This act of bestowing a surname was a significant honor, as it formally brought the individual into the ranks of the samurai. The gifting of a surname by the daimyō symbolized the new samurai's loyalty to his lord and his commitment to live by the bushidō (武士道) code. It also created a bond of vassalage, as the newly minted samurai would often take part of the daimyō's own surname, signifying their connection and service to their lord.

For example, a foot soldier (足軽, ashigaru) or lower-ranking retainer might perform such heroic deeds or demonstrate such loyalty that his lord would elevate him to the samurai class. Upon receiving his new status, the individual would often be given a new name, possibly incorporating part of his lord's surname, as a sign of his promotion. This new name would signal the samurai's new responsibilities and social rank, and he would begin to carry the daishō (大小), the two swords (katana and wakizashi) that symbolized full samurai status.

SURNAME AS A SYMBOL OF SAMURAI STATUS

Whether a samurai was born into a noble family with a hereditary surname or was granted a surname by a daimyō, the possession of a surname was essential to being recognized as a samurai. The surname was not just a marker of family lineage but also a symbol of social rank, loyalty, and responsibility within the complex hierarchy of feudal Japan.

In addition to reflecting nobility, a surname also conferred the right to engage in the responsibilities of the samurai class, including:

- Serving as a vassal to a daimyō or shogun.
- Commanding troops in battle.
- Overseeing estates and land management.
- Participating in administrative duties within a lord's domain.
- Upholding the principles of honor, loyalty, and courage that defined the samurai's way of life.

In contrast, commoners—those without surnames—were typically not permitted to rise to the ranks of the samurai, unless they were specifically elevated by a daimyō or ruler, as noted above. The possession of a surname also allowed a samurai to pass on his status to future generations, ensuring that his children would continue in the samurai tradition.

SWORDS AND SAMURAI STATUS

During the Azuchi-Momoyama period (安土桃山時代, 1573–1600), the wakizashi (脇差), a shorter sword traditionally worn alongside the katana (刀), was used not only by samurai but also by certain non-samurai individuals. While the wakizashi was an important tool for self-defense, carrying a wakizashi did not convey the prestigious status of a samurai. The distinction between samurai and non-samurai was firmly established by the katana, which served as the true symbol of the samurai class, both in terms of martial authority and social status.

USE OF THE WAKIZASHI BY NON-SAMURAI

The wakizashi was a practical weapon that could be carried by a variety of people during the Azuchi-Momoyama period, not just the samurai class. Its shorter length made it suitable for use in urban environments or confined spaces where a longer weapon like the katana would be impractical. Several groups of non-samurai individuals who frequently carried wakizashi included:

Merchants (町人, chōnin): As Japan's urban centers grew, especially during the late Sengoku and Azuchi-Momoyama periods, merchants became more influential and traveled frequently for business. While they were not part of the warrior class, some merchants were permitted to carry a wakizashi for self-defense, especially when traveling through dangerous areas. However, merchants were forbidden from carrying the longer katana, as it was a symbol of the samurai class.

Artisans (職人, shokunin): Skilled craftsmen and artisans, who were responsible for producing weapons, armor, and other items for the samurai class, often carried a wakizashi as a practical tool. This was more for utility and self-protection rather than a sign of status. Artisans were highly respected for their craft but were still lower on the social ladder than the samurai.

Doctors and Officials: Certain professionals, such as physicians or lower-ranking officials, might have been allowed to carry a wakizashi, particularly during travel. This was more for protection and convenience than as an indication of status.

Travelers and Pilgrims: Non-samurai travelers, especially those who moved between towns, might have carried a wakizashi for self-defense. Japan's roads were often dangerous, and carrying a short sword provided some protection from bandits or wild animals. However, this right was usually limited to certain situations, and the ownership of a katana remained strictly forbidden for non-samurai.

THE KATANA AS A SYMBOL OF SAMURAI STATUS

Unlike the wakizashi, the katana was the defining weapon of the samurai class, symbolizing both their social rank and their martial authority. Only samurai were permitted to carry the daishō (大小), the pairing of the katana and wakizashi. This combination of swords was not just a functional tool but a status symbol that represented the samurai's right to bear arms and enforce justice.[70]

Katana (刀): The katana was longer than the wakizashi and was considered the primary weapon of the samurai. It was a symbol of honor and power, and carrying a katana marked an individual as a member of the bushi (武士, warrior) class. The katana was seen as the embodiment of the samurai's soul, and it played an important role in rituals, ceremonies, and duels.

Ownership Restrictions: Non-samurai, regardless of wealth or influence, were not permitted to own or carry a katana. The right to carry a katana was strictly reserved for the samurai class as a sign of their social privilege. Non-samurai who violated this rule faced severe consequences, including the confiscation of the weapon and punishment, as the katana was more than just a weapon—it represented authority within the feudal system.

A central aspect of being a samurai (侍) in feudal Japan was not merely the ability to fight but the ability to navigate the complex web of political intrigue that dominated the era. While the samurai are often romanticized as fearless warriors, their role extended far beyond the battlefield. Samurai were expected to be leaders, strategists, and diplomats, rather than mere soldiers. They had to

---

[70] 大道寺友山. (1685). 武道初心集.

master the art of politics, forming alliances, managing lands, and navigating the shifting loyalties and power dynamics of the daimyō (大名) and shogun (将軍).

POLITICAL INTRIGUE AS A CORE SKILL

One of the key responsibilities of a samurai, especially those serving as vassals to powerful daimyō, was the ability to maneuver through the complex political landscape of feudal Japan. Feudal society was rife with rivalries, alliances, and betrayals, and samurai had to be adept at reading these situations to survive and thrive.

Loyalty vs. Pragmatism: Samurai were expected to show loyalty (忠義, chūgi) to their lords, but they also needed to be pragmatic in their decisions. Often, a samurai had to balance loyalty with self-preservation and the interests of their family or clan. This could involve forming temporary alliances with rivals, making strategic marriages, or even betraying a lord if it meant ensuring long-term survival or advancement.

Court Politics: High-ranking samurai were often involved in court life, advising their lords on political matters or even participating directly in diplomatic missions. Mastery of court etiquette and understanding how to influence others subtly were vital skills for samurai seeking to rise through the ranks. They had to learn how to gain the favor of higher lords or even the shogun, without appearing overly ambitious or disloyal.

Negotiation and Strategy: In many cases, samurai leaders were called upon to negotiate truces, mediate disputes, or plot complex military and political strategies. Being able to think ahead, anticipate the moves of enemies, and understand the larger geopolitical picture was a crucial part of their role. This ability to read the political landscape often determined the survival or ruin of their family or clan.

SAMURAI AS A MINORITY IN THE ARMY

While the image of the samurai as fierce warriors is accurate, it is essential to understand that samurai were a minority in the armies of feudal Japan. The bulk of the military forces during the Sengoku period (戦国時代) and the Azuchi-Momoyama period (安土桃山時代) was composed of ashigaru (足軽)—foot soldiers often recruited from the peasant class.

Samurai as Commanders: Samurai were expected to serve as commanders and leaders, not merely as foot soldiers. They were responsible for leading troops into battle, devising strategic plans, and ensuring the discipline and organization of their forces. Unlike the ashigaru, who were expected to follow orders and fight en masse, samurai were held to a higher standard of conduct and were responsible for the success or failure of military campaigns.

Delegation of Combat: While samurai were certainly skilled warriors, much of the direct combat was delegated to ashigaru. The samurai led from the front, but their role was to inspire and command, ensuring that the battle was fought according to the strategic goals of the daimyō. Their value lay not only in their ability to fight but in their capacity to lead and manage the logistics of war, including planning tactics, coordinating supply lines, and ensuring the morale of their troops.

Fearsome Reputation: Samurai were expected to embody bushidō (武士道)—the code of honor that emphasized courage, loyalty, and honor in battle. Their presence on the battlefield was symbolic, and their fearsome reputation often inspired loyalty and discipline among the lower-ranking soldiers. However, their responsibilities extended far beyond simply wielding a sword.

LAND MANAGEMENT AND LEADERSHIP

When not engaged in battle, samurai were often tasked with managing land, collecting taxes, and overseeing the daily governance of their lord's domain. This role as an administrator and leader was just as important as their military duties, as samurai were expected to maintain economic stability and ensure that their lord's territory was prosperous and well-managed.

Vassalage and Feudal Responsibilities: Many samurai acted as vassals to powerful lords, managing their fiefs and ensuring that resources such as rice, taxes, and troops were available to the daimyō in times of war. A samurai's reputation often depended on how well they managed their domain, and failure to do so could result in disgrace or loss of status.

Bureaucratic Duties: Samurai were also expected to be well-versed in the administrative duties of running a domain. This included settling legal disputes, maintaining order among the population, and ensuring that laws were enforced. While they were warriors, samurai also had to demonstrate governance skills and often acted as judges or advisors in legal matters.

YASUKE'S ROLE IN JAPAN

During the Azuchi-Momoyama period (安土桃山時代), the social structure of samurai (侍) society underwent significant changes. Traditionally, samurai status was hereditary, and only those born into established samurai families could claim the privileges and responsibilities that came with being a bushi (武士). However, the near-constant warfare of the Sengoku period (戦国時代) and the drive for unification by powerful leaders like Oda Nobunaga (織田信長) and Toyotomi Hideyoshi (豊臣 秀吉) led to an evolution in the samurai class, where merit and military service began to play a more significant role in determining samurai status.

HEREDITARY STATUS AND BIRTH

For centuries, the samurai class was primarily composed of warriors born into noble families, and lineage was the most important criterion for belonging to the bushi. The elite samurai clans, with their long-standing connections to land ownership and governance, passed down their status from one generation to the next. The maintenance of land and warrior privileges was closely tied to hereditary right.

However, with the Sengoku period's political and military upheaval, the rigid hereditary system began to loosen, especially under the leadership of figures like Oda Nobunaga.

MILITARY SERVICE AND LOYALTY

As the need for competent military commanders and warriors grew during the Azuchi-Momoyama period, military service and loyalty became crucial factors in determining who could rise to the status of samurai. The constant conflicts between warlords vying for power required the support of skilled warriors, and some of these individuals were elevated to samurai status due to their exceptional performance in battle or their unwavering loyalty to their lord.

Military commanders increasingly relied on a warrior's proven ability rather than just their ancestry. In particular, Oda Nobunaga is known for having promoted individuals based on their skills and loyalty, regardless of their background, which helped build a more diverse and capable military force.

SOCIAL MOBILITY AND MERIT-BASED PROMOTION

The elevation of Toyotomi Hideyoshi, who began his career as an ashigaru (足軽), a low-ranking foot soldier, is one of the most prominent examples of how the criteria for samurai status evolved during this period. Hideyoshi's rise through the ranks, from a commoner to becoming one of the most powerful men in Japan, illustrates the shifting nature of samurai identity. Under Hideyoshi, the strict barriers between social classes were further blurred, as he sought to consolidate power by promoting those who had demonstrated loyalty and competence.

Ōta Gyūichi (太田牛一), a contemporary of Nobunaga, documented these changes in his work 「信長公記」 *(Shinchōkōki)*, where he highlighted how Nobunaga valued talent and loyalty over the aristocratic norms of his time. Ōta writes that Nobunaga was willing to grant samurai status to individuals from humble backgrounds if they proved themselves valuable in war or governance.

Nobunaga's willingness to promote talented individuals, regardless of their birth, helped set the tone for a new kind of samurai class, one that was increasingly based on merit and performance in battle. So this raises the question, was Yasuke a samurai?

THE RIGHT TO CARRY SWORDS AND SYMBOLISM

One of the most visible symbols of samurai status was the right to carry the katana (刀) and wakizashi (脇差), the two swords that signified a warrior's social position and authority. Only those officially recognized as samurai were granted the privilege of wearing both swords, which symbolized their right to rule and serve in military leadership. The katana especially was strictly restricted to bushi class under pain of death [71]

It's important to clarify that Yasuke was given a wakizashi (脇差), not a katana (刀). This distinction is crucial because during the Sengoku (戦国) period, the mere possession of a wakizashi (脇差) did not signify samurai (侍) status. Similarly, the fact that Yasuke was granted a wakizashi (脇差) does not mean he was made a samurai (侍). At the time, wakizashi (脇差) were often practical tools carried by retainers (従者), who were responsible for the protection of their lords (主人). Retainers were typically expected to act as bodyguards, especially in volatile situations where their master could be attacked. Carrying a wakizashi (脇差) allowed these retainers to fulfill this protective role.

Yasuke, as a retainer to Oda Nobunaga (織田信長), was likely entrusted with carrying Nobunaga's personal swords like katana(刀), acting as his sword-bearer (刀持ち). It would be logical that, in addition to this responsibility, Yasuke would carry a

---

[71] Conlan, Thomas (2003). *Weapons and Fighting Techniques of the Samurai Warrior, 1200–1877 AD*. Amber Books.

wakizashi (脇差) for his own self-defense and to protect his master when necessary. The wakizashi (脇差) was often viewed as a secondary, utilitarian weapon, commonly carried by those of various social ranks. Even though it was considered an important tool, particularly for those serving as retainers, it did not denote in any way any elevated or official warrior status, such as that of a samurai (侍). At this point I risk becoming repetitive in attempting to make sure this point is clear.

To understand this fully, we need to place Yasuke's situation in the context of retainers and other non-samurai roles of the period. Yasuke's primary role as a servant and sword-bearer meant that his access to a wakizashi (脇差) was more about practicality than honor. It was not unusual for trusted servants, particularly those involved in martial service, to carry a wakizashi (脇差), as they might need to defend themselves or their lord. Thus, while modern depictions might emphasize this weapon as a symbol of Yasuke's rise to samurai (侍) status, the reality is far more grounded in the practical expectations placed on retainers during the Sengoku (戦国) period.

去程　三位中將信忠　岐阜ゟ而庭子の作靐四足作銅可被成ぃ近来之作名譽不可過之作靐師山日　齋来

兩人安土へ

寅七月廿三日　持參ぃ處右之內　一足被召上候ゟ者中將信忠へ被成作跪兩人作靐師辛勞仕たる之由　上
慇ゟて銚子五枚宛に作服相副被下色々恐備共まて讃踊い也

寅八月五日　奥州津輕之　南部宮內少輔　作靐五足進上

寅八月十日二　万見仙千代　所へ南部めし寄られ作振舞被仰付此時作體被ヤい也

寅八月十五日　江州蒲中京郡の相撲浪を初として千五百人安土へ被召留　作山まて晨剡ゟり百剡迄と
らせて作覽ぃ各我手之者共を召列られ則作奉行

作人數之事　　津田七兵衛信澄　堀久太郎　万見仙千代　村井作右衛門　木村源五　青地奥右衛門

後藤春三郎　地藏坊　布施藤九郎　蒲生忠三郎　永田刑部少輔　阿閉孫五郎

行事者　木瀬張森庵　木瀬太郎太夫　兩人也

小相撲　五番打入數之事

大相撲　三番打　人數之事

三番打（木村源五內）木村伊小介　三番打（瓦圎內）越井二兵衞尉　三番打（布施藤九郎內）山田奥兵衞

五番打（京極內ゟ江南源五　五番打（木村源五內）深尾久兵衞　五番内（布施藤九郎）者六　五番打

（久太郎内）地藏坊　五番打（後藤内）麻生三五　五番打（蒲生中間）戲下　以上

三番打（後藤內）麻生三五　三番打　長光　三番打　青地孫次　三番打　づかう　三番打　東馬二

大方相撲既及諸番　　永田刑部少輔　阿閉孫五郎　　强力之由連々被及閣食いて兩人之働作覽し度被思

食石作奉行衆之相撲作所望也初より堀久太郎　蒲生忠三郎　万見仙千代　布施藤九郎　後藤喜三郎

とられいて後又刑部少輔阿閉手相よてくまれいひ勿論阿閉器量骨柄摩れいて力のつよき事馬鹿いへと

も仕合ひ歒別强い歒刑部少輔勝相撲ゝい其日ゝ珍勳調終日取替々作相撲取ゝ被下度々能作相撲仕いゝ

ゝ付て被召出人數之事

右作相撲取被召出何れもゝのし付之太刀鞘衆作服かみ下作領中百石宛私宅等まて被仰付都鄙之面目ゝ

次第也

寅八月十七日　中將信忠　播磨より被納作馬

寅九月九日　安土作山ゝて相撲をとらせいて　中將信忠　北畠信雄卿へ作見物

九月十五日　大坂表作取出　作番衆之作目付として作小姓衆作馬廻作弓衆廿日番ゝ城ゝゝへ被相加

九月廿三日　信長公　山岡美作守所作泊次日二條作新造作參著

九月廿四日　齊藤新五　越中へ被仰付出陣開中　大田保之內作欲　權名小四郎　阿田豊

前人數入置いゝ尾濃兩國之作人數打向之由承及開落に致退散則　つけの城へ　神保越中　人數入置　群

庸新五　三里程程打出陣取いて在々所々へ相備

〔以下十四入〕

寅馬二郎　たいそう　づから　妙仁　ひし屋　助五郎　水原孫太郎　大塚新八　わら鹿　山田與兵

衛　圓淨寺源七　村田吉五　蒲生三五　靑地孫治

篇　三番打　たいそう　三番打　圓淨寺源七　三番打　大塚新八　三番打　ひし屋　〔以上〕

There are some who argue that Yasuke (弥助) was recognized as a samurai simply because Nobunaga (信長) gave him a wakizashi, a residence, and a stipend. It should be pointed out that Nobunaga regularly rewarded people he favored in this manner. For example,

142

on August 15, 1578 (天正 6 年 8 月 15 日), three years before Yasuke entered Nobunaga's service, Nobunaga summoned 1,500 sumo wrestlers (相撲取り) from Kyoto (京都) and Ōmi Province (江州) to perform in Azuchi (安土). On that day, he granted 14 of the wrestlers swords with ceremonial cords, formal attire, and a stipend of 100 koku (扶持 100 石) each, along with private residences (私宅).

The relevant passage from the Shinchō Kōki (信長公記, Chronicle of Lord Nobunaga) states:
"Those summoned to the sumo match were awarded swords with ceremonial cords (熨斗つき太刀脇差), formal attire (裃), and 100 koku each, along with private residences. This brought great honor to both the urban and rural areas (都鄙)."

So, are we to assume that these 14 sumo wrestlers, who received more than Yasuke did, were also recognized as samurai within the Oda clan (織田家)? That would not make much sense.

The Shinchō Kōki (信長公記, Volume 11)[72] even lists their names: Taitō (たいとう), Zukau (づかう), Myōjin (妙仁), Hishiya (ひし屋), Suke Gorō (助五郎), Arashika (あら鹿) with

---

[72] 信長公記　巻 11

143

many of them not having proper surnames, just sumo-style names (しこ名).

Despite receiving more prestigious gifts than Yasuke, would this elevate these sumo wrestlers to the rank of samurai or something similar? Obviously not.

The notion that Yasuke's possession of a wakizashi (脇差) indicated he was a samurai (侍) has been exaggerated in some modern accounts. This interpretation seems to come from a misunderstanding of the social hierarchies and roles during the period. The wakizashi (脇差) was a weapon used by a wide range of people, including those who were never part of the bushi (武士) class. Just as merchants and doctors could carry this weapon without being elevated to warrior status, Yasuke's possession of a wakizashi (脇差) was a functional part of his duties rather than a mark of promotion to the warrior class.

A FAMILY NAME

One of the strongest indicators that Yasuke (弥助) was not a samurai (侍) is the glaring absence of any historical record documenting him being given a last name (姓). In the Sengoku (戦国) period, receiving a last name was a critical and formal prerequisite for anyone to become a samurai (侍). Nobunaga (織田

144

信長), or any other powerful lord, would have granted a surname to someone who was elevated to samurai (侍) status, as it signified their entry into the bushi (武士) class and, by extension, into the upper echelons of the warrior aristocracy. There are no examples of samurai (侍) without surnames in this period. Therefore, if Yasuke had truly been made a samurai (侍), a significant part of that process would have been Nobunaga granting him a Japanese surname (苗字).

It is important to recognize that such an event, especially with someone as high-profile and unique as Yasuke, would have caused a considerable stir at the time. A non-Japanese, foreign-born servant being elevated to samurai (侍) status, and being bestowed a surname, would have been seen as an extraordinary event. Given Yasuke's uniqueness as a foreign servant, the granting of a samurai (侍) name to him would likely have been viewed as a significant event worthy of detailed documentation. Historians and chroniclers, particularly those close to Nobunaga such as Ōta Gyūichi (太田牛一), who meticulously recorded events in Nobunaga's life, would have surely made note of it in their writings. Ōta (太田) recorded many details about Nobunaga's retainers, their ranks, and their status changes, yet there is nothing indicating that Yasuke was given a surname or officially promoted to samurai (侍) status.[73]

The historical silence on this matter is itself a powerful statement. The fact that no record exists of Yasuke receiving a surname suggests that such an event never occurred. The absence of such an important detail in the historical texts, including accounts from close contemporaries like Ōta Gyūichi (太田牛一) and Jesuit sources, speaks volumes. It's especially telling because historians of the period were diligent in recording any unusual or significant changes in status, particularly involving someone as distinctive as Yasuke.

Moreover, the lack of a surname for Yasuke undermines the narrative that he was ever formally made a samurai (侍). The process of becoming a samurai (侍) was a formal, social, and legal transformation that could not be overlooked or left unrecorded. The fact that Yasuke is never referred to with a surname in any surviving records of the time strongly suggests that he remained a servant, perhaps a retainer (従者) at most, but not a samurai (侍). This historical "deafening silence," where no records detail

[73]Ota, G., Elisonas, J. S., & Lamers, J. P. (2011). Book I Ōta Izumi No Kami Composed This. And It Records The Life Of Lord Oda Danjō No Jō Nobunaga From Eiroku 11 [1568], The Year Of Earth Senior And The Dragon. In *The Chronicle of Lord Nobunaga* (pp. 116-127). Brill.

Yasuke's supposed promotion or the granting of a surname, counts heavily against the idea that he was ever elevated to the samurai (侍) class.

Receiving a house and a stipend was fairly common for retainers during the Sengoku period, and it does not necessarily imply samurai (侍) status. Many retainers, especially those who provided personal service to a daimyō (大名) or lord, were granted a stipend and living accommodations, but this was a standard practice even for non-samurai (侍) servants of certain ranks. In the case of Yasuke (弥助), receiving a stipend from Nobunaga (織田信長) indicates that he was not being treated as a slave, but rather as a servant within Nobunaga's household.

Receiving a stipend, therefore, reflects his integration into Nobunaga's retinue as a trusted servant. The stipend would have provided him with the means to live independently, distinguishing him from a slave, who would not receive such payments or autonomy. This further implies that Yasuke was likely freed from slavery before entering Nobunaga's service. It is probable that the Jesuits (イエズス会), who initially brought Yasuke to Japan, may have played a role in releasing him from bondage, either formally or informally. Alternatively, it is also possible that Yasuke had secured his own freedom prior to joining the Jesuits, which would explain his shift from being viewed as property to being regarded as a retainer in Japan.

However, this does not suggest that Yasuke was elevated to the rank of samurai (侍). Many servants or retainers, including personal doctors (医師) to daimyō , received stipends, but this did not grant them samurai (侍) status. Rather, it positioned them as important members of a lord's household, yet still subordinate to the actual warrior class.

A NOVELTY

Nobunaga (織田信長) was well known for his fascination with foreign goods and cultures, and he often sought to display his wealth and connections through these exotic items as status symbols which was a common practice of the powerful at the time[74]. Historical records show that Nobunaga went to great lengths to acquire rare foreign products, such as firearms, textiles, and other items brought to Japan by European traders, particularly the Portuguese. This interest extended beyond material goods to people, as having foreign retainers in his service was also a way for Nobunaga to showcase his status and power.

---

[74] Yazıcıoğlu, E. T. (1996). *A Historical Analysis of Consumer Culture in Japan: Momoyama-Genroku (1573-1703)* (Master's thesis, Bilkent Universitesi (Turkey)).

In Yasuke's (弥助) case, being an "exotic" foreigner, specifically an African in a land where most people had likely never seen someone with his appearance, made him a unique figure in Nobunaga's retinue. By keeping Yasuke as a retainer, Nobunaga could present him as a kind of living symbol of his influence and his connections with foreign powers. The presence of a foreigner in his household was a powerful statement to his rivals and other daimyō (大名), signaling that Nobunaga had access to rare and valuable resources, even human ones. Yasuke's presence served as a display of Nobunaga's broad reach and his ability to acquire and control things from beyond Japan's borders.

It's also important to note that Nobunaga was known for his innovative and unconventional strategies, which included aligning himself with the Jesuits and other foreign entities for tactical advantage. Having Yasuke in his court would have added to this image of being open to new ideas and influences, further setting him apart from more traditional daimyō (大名) who might have been more insular in their approach.

However, beyond the prestige and status that came with having Yasuke as a retainer, it is unlikely that Yasuke was primarily valued for his abilities as a warrior or protector. While Yasuke may have served as a bodyguard or sword-bearer, the symbolic value of having an African retainer likely outweighed any practical military benefits he might have provided. Yasuke's role would have been more about enhancing Nobunaga's image as a cosmopolitan and powerful leader, rather than his military prowess.

In this way, Yasuke functioned not just as a retainer or servant but also as a status symbol, much like the foreign goods that Nobunaga so famously prized. The daimyō (大名) in Japan often competed with one another to showcase their wealth, power, and influence, and having Yasuke, a highly unusual and striking figure, would have been a potent display of Nobunaga's prestige.

TRAINING AS SAMURAI

Yasuke (弥助) was in Japan for a relatively short period, which makes it highly improbable that he had the time necessary to become a samurai (侍) in the traditional sense. The process of becoming a samurai was long and rigorous, often taking years of intense training and discipline to master the various skills required for such a status.

SAMURAI TRAINING AND TIME REQUIREMENTS

Traditionally, a samurai had to be proficient in several weapons and combat techniques, including:

1. Katana (刀) - The iconic samurai sword.
2. Yari (槍) - Spear fighting, essential for battlefield combat.

3. Kyūjutsu (弓術) - Archery, a key skill for both infantry and cavalry samurai.

4. Naginata (薙刀) - A pole weapon often used by both samurai and their retainers.

5. Horsemanship (騎馬術) - Skilled riding, crucial for mounted warriors.

6. Jujutsu (柔術) - Unarmed combat and grappling techniques.

Young men destined to become samurai typically began training in these disciplines from a very early age, often as young as five or six. This training was continuous, with years spent honing each of the necessary skills before they could even consider being formally recognized as samurai.

YASUKE'S LIMITED TIME IN JAPAN

Yasuke's time in Japan, by historical accounts, was brief. He arrived in Japan in 1579 with the Jesuit missionary Alessandro Valignano, and his service to Oda Nobunaga (織田信長) likely began around 1581. His time in Nobunaga's service ended with Nobunaga's death at the Honnō-ji Incident (本能寺の変) in June 1582. This gives Yasuke at most three years in Japan, with only around a year and a half to two years in Nobunaga's service.

This short timeframe makes it almost impossible for Yasuke to have undergone the extensive training required to become a samurai. Unlike ashigaru (足軽, foot soldiers), who might be quickly trained for basic infantry duties, samurai were expected to be highly skilled in multiple forms of combat, as mentioned above. Foreign samurai were extremely rare and even then, it took many years of training as can be seen in the example of the ethnically Korean samurai Wakita Kyūbei (脇田 九兵衛: 1585–1660)[75] became samurai only after spending the majority of his childhood being trained in martial arts and samurai etiquette along with fighting in many battles.[76]

Yasuke simply did not have the time necessary to master these skills to the level expected of a full-fledged samurai.

THE DISTINCTION BETWEEN SAMURAI AND FOOT SOLDIERS

It's also important to understand that samurai were distinct from other military ranks such as ashigaru. While ashigaru were often conscripted from the peasantry and given basic training with spears

---

[75] Wakita Kyūbei (1585–1660), served under the famous warlord Maeda Toshinaga (前田 利長) who lived during the Azuchi-Momoyama period (1573–1600) and the early Edo period (1603–1868)

[76] Nelson, D. (2021). From Erstwhile Captive to Cultural Erudite: The Career of Korean-Born Samurai, Wakita Kyūbei. In *The Power of the Dispersed* (pp. 285-310). Brill.

or arquebuses (matchlock guns), samurai were members of the warrior class who were trained not only in combat but also in the cultural and ethical codes such as bushidō (武士道). Samurai were expected to live by a strict code of honor, and their social status was significantly higher than that of regular soldiers.

The rigorous process of becoming a samurai and mastering multiple weapons made it highly unlikely that Yasuke could have achieved such a status in his short time in Japan. Even though he was entrusted with a wakizashi (脇差, short sword), this does not make him a samurai. At the time, even non-samurai individuals such as merchants, doctors, and officials were permitted to carry a wakizashi for self-defense. As a retainer, Yasuke would likely have been given the wakizashi as a practical tool to protect Nobunaga and himself if needed, not as a symbol of his induction into the samurai class.

A QUESTION OF LANGUAGE SKILL

One significant issue that often goes overlooked in discussions about Yasuke (弥助) is his ability to speak Japanese. Many modern accounts seem to inflate or misunderstand how well Yasuke could communicate in Japanese, which is important because achieving fluency in a language, especially as complex as Japanese, typically takes several years of dedicated study, even with modern language learning resources and full-time instruction. Yasuke, however, had none of these advantages.

TIME REQUIRED TO LEARN JAPANESE FLUENTLY

In today's world, it's estimated that achieving fluency in Japanese for an English speaker takes around 2,200 hours of dedicated study, according to the Foreign Service Institute (FSI). This translates to approximately 88 weeks, or nearly two years of full-time, intensive language learning under optimal conditions—using modern language tools such as textbooks, immersive environments, native-speaking tutors, and digital resources.

Yasuke, by contrast, had none of these modern resources. We don't know how much time he had to study Japanese or whether he received any formal instruction at all. While it's possible that the Jesuits may have taught him some basic Japanese, the historical record does not specify the extent of his education, nor do we have any direct evidence that he could read or write in any language, let alone Japanese.

ILLITERACY AS A BARRIER TO LANGUAGE LEARNING

Given that Yasuke had a background in slavery, it is very likely that he could have been illiterate. In many cultures, slaves were rarely taught to read or write, as literacy was seen as unnecessary or even dangerous in maintaining control over enslaved populations. This could have drastically affected his ability to learn Japanese quickly, as literacy generally aids in faster language acquisition.

Even if the Jesuits (イエズス会) did teach Yasuke some basic literacy, there is no surviving record to confirm whether or not this happened. Thus, any claim that Yasuke was literate—or illiterate—remains speculative. Without written evidence or confirmation of his literacy in any language, it is difficult to gauge how quickly he might have been able to pick up Japanese, a language with a notoriously difficult writing system that includes kanji (漢字), hiragana (ひらがな), and katakana (カタカナ).

PRACTICAL BARRIERS TO YASUKE'S LANGUAGE LEARNING

The other factor to consider is Yasuke's short time in Japan, which, as mentioned earlier, was only about two to three years. Even if he had some limited exposure to Japanese before arriving with the Jesuits, learning Japanese proficiently within this timeframe would have been incredibly difficult, especially given his responsibilities as a retainer (従者) to Nobunaga (織田信長). Yasuke's time was likely consumed by the daily duties of a servant and retainer, leaving him little opportunity for dedicated language study.

Further complicating this issue is that historical accounts indicate that Yasuke spoke "a little Japanese." The Jesuit records describe Nobunaga's interest in Yasuke because he could speak some Japanese, but the phrase used in the Jesuit Annual Reports (イエズ ス会日本年報) is "少しく日本語を解した"—which simply means "he understood a little Japanese." This suggests a very basic level of comprehension, rather than fluency. The fact that this specific phrase is used indicates that Yasuke was far from fluent and that any extensive communication he had with Nobunaga would have been limited.

OVERSTATED JAPANESE ABILITY

Given the evidence, it's unlikely that Yasuke had more than a rudimentary grasp of Japanese, let alone the level of fluency needed to function as a samurai (侍), a role that required not just combat skills but also participation in complex social, legal, and military discussions. His potential illiteracy, the lack of formal resources, and the limited time he spent in Japan all strongly suggest that his language abilities have been overstated in modern retellings of his story. The speculation about Yasuke's Japanese ability and the larger issues surrounding his communication skills will be discussed in more detail in a later chapter.

SKILL AS A COMMANDER

Yasuke's limited proficiency in the Japanese language significantly undermines the claim that he was a samurai (侍), especially given the high demands of communication required for such a role. The historical record indicates that Yasuke "spoke a little Japanese," which suggests only a basic ability to interact in the language. In contrast, the role of a samurai involved far more than just physical prowess; it required leadership, tactical understanding, and clear communication, particularly during battles or high-stakes situations.

SAMURAI AND THE NEED FOR ADVANCED COMMUNICATION

The samurai (侍) were not just warriors—they were also leaders and strategists, often responsible for commanding groups of soldiers, issuing orders, and making rapid decisions in the heat of battle. Communication was essential for these tasks. Samurai were expected to understand and give commands fluently, make strategic decisions in real-time, and relay those commands clearly to those under their command. This level of interaction required fluency not only in spoken Japanese but also a deep understanding of cultural and hierarchical nuances that are integral to the language.

In a battle situation, miscommunication could lead to disastrous results, including the loss of life, failed strategies, and defeat. A person with limited Japanese proficiency, like Yasuke, would have posed a significant risk in such a role. It is hard to imagine how someone who could only speak "a little Japanese" could effectively lead troops or relay complex commands in the midst of combat, especially during a time when quick thinking and immediate action were required.

YASUKE'S ROLE: SWORD BEARER, NOT SAMURAI

The historical evidence points toward Yasuke serving primarily as a sword bearer (従者) or retainer for Oda Nobunaga (織田信長), not as a full-fledged samurai (侍). This position involved carrying Nobunaga's swords and being close to him, particularly in ceremonial or symbolic contexts. The task of carrying a daimyō's (大名) swords did not require the extensive language skills or leadership capabilities that were expected of samurai. In this capacity, Yasuke would only need to understand basic commands or instructions, and even then, the Jesuit translators would likely have assisted him in more complex interactions.

Being a sword bearer did not necessitate the extensive training and expertise in weaponry, tactics, or the broader skill set that the samurai possessed. Sword bearers, while important, were not considered leaders in the way samurai were. Their primary function was to serve and protect their master, and this task could largely be fulfilled with basic physical strength and loyalty—qualities Yasuke undoubtedly possessed. The limited language proficiency he had would have been sufficient for this role, where understanding simple commands was enough, and direct involvement in battle strategy or troop management was unnecessary.

LANGUAGE PROFICIENCY: A MAJOR OBSTACLE TO THE SAMURAI CLAIM

To become a samurai, one not only needed to be skilled in combat but also fluent in Japanese, particularly because they would interact with fellow samurai, daimyō (大名), and various subordinates in the chain of command. Yasuke's inability to speak Japanese fluently is a critical flaw in the argument that he was a samurai. Had Yasuke been granted the rank of samurai, his responsibilities would have gone far beyond merely being in close proximity to Nobunaga (信長). He would have needed to demonstrate proficiency with multiple weapons, command troops, and act as a decision-maker in the highly complex and hierarchical world of samurai warfare.

A SAVIOR OF THE PEOPLE?

Another glaring issue with the portrayal of Yasuke in popular media is the romanticized narrative that casts him as a liberator of the Japanese peasantry while in the service of Oda Nobunaga (織田信長). This image is not only historically inaccurate but also presents a distorted understanding of the realities of Yasuke's time and the role he played in Nobunaga's regime.

Far from being a liberator, Yasuke worked for a daimyō (大名) who was infamous for his subjugation of the people. Nobunaga was not driven by ideals of freedom or justice for the common folk; rather, his singular ambition was to expand his influence and ultimately unite Japan under his rule, often through brutal means. Nobunaga was ruthless in his pursuit of power, and historical accounts paint a clear picture of his readiness to commit atrocities against civilians if it helped further his aims. This is a far cry from the "benevolent liberator" image that some portrayals attempt to impose on Nobunaga, and by extension, on Yasuke as his servant.

NOBUNAGA: A RUTHLESS LEADER

Nobunaga's (信長) subjugation of the Japanese people is well documented. For instance, during the Siege of Mount Hiei (比叡山焼き討ち) in 1571, Nobunaga ordered the massacre of thousands of Buddhist monks, women, and children at Enryaku-ji (延暦寺)

on Mount Hiei. This was done not because the civilians posed a direct threat to his military might, but because they symbolized resistance to his authority. The massacre sent a clear message to his enemies about the lengths Nobunaga was willing to go to in order to eliminate obstacles to his rule. Such actions reveal the darker, more tyrannical side of Nobunaga's leadership, where the slaughter of civilians was seen as an acceptable means to gain territory or secure power.[77]

In other battles, Nobunaga demonstrated a similar disregard for civilian life, such as the Ishiyama Hongan-ji War (石山合戦), in which his forces besieged and destroyed the stronghold of the Ikkō-ikki (一向一揆), a sect of warrior monks and peasants who resisted his control. The suppression of this group further underscores Nobunaga's determination to crush any opposition to his rule, even when it involved devastating civilian populations.

YASUKE'S ROLE: SERVING A TYRANT, NOT A LIBERATOR

Yasuke's portrayal as some kind of liberator or hero for the oppressed masses of Japan is ironic given the fact that he served a daimyō whose actions were far from liberating. Rather than being

---

[77] Tsang, C. R. (2020). *War and Faith: Ikkō Ikki in Late Muromachi Japan* (Vol. 288). BRILL.

a champion of the peasantry, Yasuke worked for a leader who often exploited and brutalized civilians for political and territorial gain. Yasuke's role in Nobunaga's court was primarily that of a retainer and sword bearer. There is no historical evidence to suggest that Yasuke was in any way involved in liberating peasants or resisting the oppression of the common people.

In fact, the idea of Yasuke as a champion of the people is a completely modern invention, fueled by narratives that seek to romanticize his story. Yasuke, as a servant of Nobunaga, was part of a system that supported Nobunaga's rule—one that was characterized by the consolidation of power through military conquest and subjugation of any who stood in the way. Far from challenging the status quo, Yasuke was part of the retinue of a man who sought to expand and secure his dominion over all of Japan, regardless of the cost to its people.

NOBUNAGA'S MIXED LEGACY

To be clear, Nobunaga (信長) was not without his merits when compared to his contemporaries. He is often credited with implementing reforms that paved the way for the eventual unification of Japan under Toyotomi Hideyoshi (豊臣秀吉) and Tokugawa Ieyasu (徳川家康). He promoted meritocracy in his ranks, reducing the rigid class structures of the time, and encouraged trade and technological advancements, particularly through his openness to foreign influence.[78]

However, these advancements do not obscure the fact that Nobunaga was, at heart, a power-hungry daimyō who prioritized his own ambition over the welfare of the people. His use of military force to expand his territories, his strategic use of violence, and his disregard for civilian life make it clear that he was far from the image of a benevolent ruler or liberator.

YASUKE: A RETAINER, NOT A REVOLUTIONARY

Yasuke's short time in Japan and his relatively limited role in Nobunaga's court further diminishes any notion of him as a liberator or protector of the Japanese people. The narrative that casts Yasuke as a revolutionary figure liberating the oppressed masses is a product of modern wishful thinking not historical reality.

A LACK OF INFORMATION

As I delve deeper into the life of Yasuke, I find myself constantly grappling with a fundamental issue: the scarcity of historical records. The more research I conduct, the clearer it becomes that

---

[78] Inoguchi, T. (1997). The Japanese political system: Its basic continuity in historical perspective. *Asian Journal of Political Science*, 5(2), 65-77.

much of what is widely believed about Yasuke—his life, his supposed accomplishments, and his status—are not rooted in historical fact but are largely the products of modern romanticization and mythmaking.

It's a strange position to be in as an author. One would think that the life of a figure as intriguing as Yasuke, a rare African retainer to one of Japan's most powerful warlords, would be rich with documented events and verifiable historical milestones. Yet, the opposite is true. The historical sources that do mention Yasuke provide only fleeting glimpses of his life, offering a handful of verifiable facts, but leaving enormous gaps in his story. These gaps, unfortunately, have been filled not with careful scholarship but with hyperactive imaginations.

Popular media, in particular, has played a significant role in transforming Yasuke from a historical figure into a larger-than-life legend. His story has been inflated to include fantastical elements, such as being a powerful samurai, liberating the oppressed, or playing a key role in major historical events. The reality, however, is far more subdued. Yasuke's time in Japan was brief, and the historical record does not support many of the grandiose claims made about him.

Much of what we know comes from sparse and often ambiguous sources, like the Jesuit reports (イエズス会年報) or the writings of Ōta Gyūichi (太田牛一), which mention Yasuke only in passing. These records describe his role as a retainer and sword bearer but give no indication of the dramatic exploits that later narratives have attributed to him. There is no mention of him becoming a samurai, no evidence of heroic battles, and no clear documentation of his personal life or background.

As a researcher, it's both frustrating and fascinating to observe how these embellishments have taken on a life of their own, spreading through popular culture and even seeping into what some consider to be historical accounts. The truth, it seems, is far less sensational—Yasuke was a foreign retainer who likely served as a status symbol for Oda Nobunaga (織田信長), a rare and exotic figure in a court that valued such displays. Beyond that, the details of his life remain shrouded in mystery.

For those seeking a gripping tale of a foreigner rising through the ranks of the samurai, Yasuke's story may seem disappointingly lacking in drama. But to me, this scarcity of information speaks volumes about the ways in which history and myth intertwine. As I continue to write, I feel compelled to separate fact from fiction, to resist the temptation to embellish the narrative for the sake of a more compelling story. It's a difficult task, especially when so little is known for certain. Yet, it's a task worth undertaking, as the true story of Yasuke, while less glamorous, remains an important part of history—one that deserves to be told with accuracy and care, even if that means acknowledging that we may never know the full picture.[79]

In the end, the challenge isn't that there's too little to write about Yasuke; it's that we must sift through the noise and recognize how much of what has been written about him is simply fiction dressed up as history.

[79] 高橋 寛次 (2024) 弥助問題「本人は芸人のような立場」「日本人の不満は当然」 歴史学者・呉座氏に聞く（上）
https://www.sankei.com/article/20240805-2RDCMCMKMNFYFOGXMRGPCIT2NI/

PROBLEMS IN "AFRICAN SAMURAI"

There are problems with the interpretation of some of the historical records especially in large portions of Thomas Lockley's work "African Samurai". The first recorded meeting between Oda Nobunaga and Yasuke, as frequently dramatized, happened when Father Organtino brought a black man (*cafre*)[80] to meet Nobunaga, who had specifically requested the encounter. This contradicts many fictional portrayals where Valignano (ヴァリニャーノ神

---

[80] We can guess that Yasuke was Southeast Africa because the term Cafre (from Arabic كافر kāfir, meaning "infidel" or "non-believer") was primarily used by the Portuguese during the Age of Exploration to refer to people from Southeast Africa, particularly Bantu-speaking groups. The word Cafre was used to describe people along the eastern coast of Africa, especially in Mozambique, as well as other parts of the Indian Ocean like Madagascar. In contrast, when referring to people from India, the Portuguese typically used terms like "Gentio" (for Hindus, from Latin gentilis, meaning "pagan" or "heathen"), "Mouro" (for Muslims, from Latin Maurus, meaning "Moor"), and "Malabar" (for people from the southwestern coastal region of India, particularly Kerala). They also used more specific terms to describe different regional and religious communities in India, but Cafre was not applied to Indians.

167

父) is often shown present, even though historical records suggest that Valignano was not present during this initial encounter. Nobunaga's excitement and the proximity of the Jesuit mission (*Namban-dera*, 南蛮寺)—only about a five-minute walk from Nobunaga's residence at Honno-ji (本能寺)—may explain why Nobunaga called for Yasuke so quickly. The sight of the *cafre* caused a stir, as people gathered to catch a glimpse, and it's possible that Nobunaga's impatience led to a less formal first meeting.

The second meeting was a more official occasion. Father Valignano, along with Father Organtino and Luis Frois (ルイスフロイス), visited Nobunaga and brought gifts such as a golden chair (*cadeira dourada*) and crimson velvet (*vidro christalino*).[81] Despite the elaborate nature of the gifts, there is no mention of Yasuke or any other *cafre* in the record, and he does not appear on the list of offerings presented during this visit.

In the "Shinchō Kōki" (信長公記), a historical chronicle of Nobunaga's life, two separate events from February 23rd were merged into one. These were the arrival of a black monk (*kuro-bōzu*, 黒坊主) from the Christian territories and the formal visit

---

[81] Luis Frois, S. J. *The First European Description of Japan, 1585.* Routledge.

from the Jesuits (*bateren-shōretsu*, 伴天連召列参). The decision to combine these two distinct incidents likely came from an attempt to avoid narrative confusion. However, the result is a more streamlined but less detailed version of the events.

This tendency to conflate events for storytelling purposes has persisted. Modern retellings of Yasuke's story often borrow from Valignano's interactions with Nobunaga, such as Nobunaga's surprise at Valignano's height and the lengthy conversations they reportedly had. These details, although not related to Yasuke, have been woven into his legend, embellishing the historical facts.

A lesser-known story from Luis Frois provides another glimpse of Yasuke, or possibly another African, about a month after the initial meeting with Nobunaga. Frois recounts how, during a journey to Echizen (越前) to visit Shibata Katsuie (柴田勝家), the Jesuits passed through Nagahama. Upon arriving at the local lord's residence, crowds tried to break through the gates multiple times to see the *cafre* traveling with Frois and Valignano. The record states:

"其家に着いて、主人は群集の入ることを防ぐ爲め戸を閉ぢたが、三、四回之を破って家に入り、同伴した黒奴を見んとした" (Upon arriving at the house, the host closed the gates to prevent the crowd from entering, but they broke in three or four times to see the accompanying black man.) [82]

This is a rare mention of a *cafre* during that trip, but after this brief note, the *cafre* is not mentioned again. This leaves open the question: was this individual Yasuke, or was it another black man in their company? It's uncertain, as no additional information is provided in Frois's later reports.

If Yasuke had already entered Nobunaga's service by this time, it would seem odd for him to still be traveling with the Jesuits, which raises the possibility that the *cafre* mentioned was someone else. Valignano might have brought multiple black servants to Japan, though the records don't explicitly support this. The phrase *"cafre que traziamos"* (the *cafre* we brought) could imply that the rumors had traveled faster than the actual *cafre*, reaching Nagahama before the Jesuits did. It is also possible that Frois confused events from other parts of the trip, blending different details into one report.

Despite popular stories, there is no record in which Nobunaga expresses particular amazement at Yasuke's height. Instead, historical records, including one from Frois, state that Nobunaga was struck by Valignano's tall stature: *"espantou-se não pouco de*

---

[82] Luis Frois, "Jesuit Annual Report" (耶蘇会の日本年報), May 19, 1581.

170

sua grande estatura" (he was not a little astonished by his great height). Likewise, the idea that Nobunaga "loved talking to Yasuke" appears to stem from a misinterpretation. The original Portuguese reads:

"assi não se fartava de o ver muitas vezes, & falar com elle, por que sabia mediocremente a lingoa de Iapaõ" (He did not tire of seeing him many times and speaking with him because he knew a little Japanese).

This was likely misunderstood during translation. Rather than indicating that Nobunaga had an insatiable desire to converse with Yasuke, it simply notes that Nobunaga spoke with him once or twice because Yasuke could communicate in basic Japanese. The embellishment that Nobunaga was fascinated with Yasuke appears to be a modern invention, possibly from over-interpretation of limited historical sources.

On the other hand, the records show that Nobunaga was deeply engaged in conversations with Valignano, as indicated by:

"長時間種々の事に付いて語つた" (They spoke for a long time on various topics) — Luis Frois, April 14, 1581.

This highlights that Nobunaga's interest lay more with Valignano than with Yasuke.

Lastly, while Frois's account of the *cafre* in Nagahama is intriguing, it leaves many questions unanswered. We can't say for certain if this was Yasuke or another African, nor do we know what role Yasuke may have played at this time. Further historical research may shed light on these mysteries, but for now, the records remain inconclusive. The actual recorded interaction between Nobunaga and Yasuke is only a brief note in the records.

A QUESTION OF HEIGHT

YASUKE'S HEIGHT: THE INITIAL SOURCE IN *IETADA NIKKI*

The earliest known reference to Yasuke's height comes from the Japanese chronicle *Ietada Nikki* (『家忠日記』), written by Matsudaira Ietada (松平家忠), a retainer of Tokugawa Ieyasu. In the entry, Yasuke's height is noted as "六尺二分" (6 shaku 2 bu), which, when converted, translates to approximately 182 cm (about 6 feet). This is an unusually precise measurement, especially given that Ietada likely didn't personally measure Yasuke. Despite this, the detail is significant because it is the only known primary source recording Yasuke's height.

Yet, this precise measurement has sparked debate. Some historians believe that the use of the unit "bu" (2 bu = 6 shaku 2 bu = 182 cm) is overly exact and may have been a mistake, or perhaps an exaggeration. Other contemporaneous figures, such as Portuguese missionary Alessandro Valignano, were also noted for their height, but no similar precision is applied to them. The *Ietada Nikki* record seems to stand alone in its specificity.

A theory exists that the mention of "six shaku two bu" for Yasuke may not be a coincidence. In fact, *Ietada Nikki* also mentions a mermaid (人魚) with the exact same height in another entry, leading some to speculate that the measurement might have been applied symbolically or exaggerated for dramatic effect.

This kind of oddly specific measurement raises questions. In literature and historical records from that time, the use of "six shaku two bu" seems to be highly concentrated and mostly appears in fictional or legendary contexts, often describing larger-than-life characters. A search for other uses of "six shaku two bu" in historical texts reveals a distinct pattern. For example, in *Soga Monogatari* (曽我物語),[83] the warrior Matano Gorō Kagehisa (俣野五郎景久) is described with a height of "six shaku two bu" and a "dark complexion" (色浅黒く). Similarly, the famous warrior monk Musashibō Benkei (武蔵坊弁慶), who appears in the

---

[83] Ichiko, T. (市古 貞次). (1966). *Soga Monogatari* (曽我物語). Iwanami Shoten.

Kōwakamai play *Togashi* (『富樫』), is also described as having the same height and a "dark complexion" (色黒く).

In another example, the legendary figure Oguri Hangan (小栗判官), featured in medieval stories, is said to have been revived at a hot spring to his original height of "six shaku two bu." Lastly, Kagawa Katsuo (香川勝雄), a warlord from Aki Province during the Sengoku period, is described as "six shaku eight bu" (六尺八分) with a dark complexion in *Intoku Taiheiki* (『陰徳太平記』),[84] linking the use of specific measurements with larger-than-life and often dark-skinned characters.

From these examples, it becomes clear that "six shaku two bu" might not have been a literal measurement taken from Yasuke but rather a figure used in literature to describe particularly tall and dark-skinned individuals. This description might have been an idiomatic expression borrowed from earlier legends and applied to Yasuke, whose height and dark skin were likely to leave a strong impression. In this context, Yasuke's height might have been exaggerated to fit a narrative rather than reflect his actual size.

Looking further into *Ietada Nikki*, it becomes apparent that its recording of Yasuke's height may have been influenced by the

---

[84] Kagawa, S. (香川 宣阿). (1717). *Intoku Taiheiki* (『陰徳太平記』)

author's familiarity with other stories. For instance, the diary also contains references to plays such as *Togashi*, where Benkei, described as "six shaku two bu," performs.[85] It's likely that Ietada, who had knowledge of such legendary figures, borrowed this description when writing about Yasuke.

Hence, recorded height of Yasuke in *Ietada Nikki* may not be a precise physical measurement but rather a literary trope used to describe other towering, dark-skinned figures. This suggests that the historical record might have been more about framing Yasuke within familiar cultural narratives rather than providing an accurate account of his physical traits.

The fact that *Yamaoka Tesshū* (山岡鉄舟), a notable figure from the Bakumatsu period, was recorded to be 6 shaku 2 sun (188 cm) tall suggests that even during the Sengoku period, when Yasuke is said to have been around 182 cm, there were certainly individuals who were taller than him. The average height of people during the Sengoku period was likely higher than it was during the late Edo period, so Yasuke's height, while remarkable, would not have made him completely unique in terms of stature. Therefore, it's likely that Yasuke wasn't necessarily the tallest person around, and

---

[85] Matsudaira, I. (松平 家忠). (1966). *Ietada Nikki* (『家忠日記』). Tokyo: Daiichi Shobō. Covers his journals for 17-year interval between 1575 and August 1594

there may have been other individuals of similar or even greater height during that time.

Figure 1Yamaoka Tesshū (山岡鉄舟)

The mythological narrative surrounding Yasuke, provides a compelling case of how circular reporting can perpetuate inaccuracies, creating a distorted historical record. This circular referencing process can be traced back to a single source of misinformation, which is then copied and cited across various platforms without any verification, giving the false appearance of reliability. In Yasuke's case, the details regarding his height and skin color became central points of this feedback loop, with media outlets, academic sources, and even fact-checked platforms perpetuating these myths. Let's delve into the chronology of how these inaccuracies were created and spread.

WIKIPEDIA: THE ORIGIN OF THE MISINTERPRETATION

Fast forward to 2006, when Yasuke's height first appeared on the English Wikipedia page. The page stated that Yasuke's height was 6 shaku 2 sun (approximately 188 cm), not the original 6 shaku 2 bu. This misinterpretation likely stemmed from a misunderstanding of the difference between "bu" and "sun." The unit "sun" is larger (1 sun = 3 cm), so changing "bu" to "sun" inflated Yasuke's height from 182 cm to 188 cm. It is unclear whether this was an intentional exaggeration or a simple mistake, but it became the first point of confusion in the narrative.

THE SPREAD OF THE 188 CM MYTH

From this misinterpreted Wikipedia entry, the idea that Yasuke was 188 cm tall began to spread. By 2013, the Wikipedia page still reflected this incorrect figure, and the description of Yasuke's height started being picked up by various other sources.

- In 2013, a website called *yasuke-san.com* included the same measurement, writing that Yasuke was "6 shaku 2 sun (188 cm)," repeating the Wikipedia error almost verbatim.
- In 2019, a *BBC* article titled *"Yasuke: The Mysterious African Samurai"* repeated this height: "His height was 6 shaku 2 sun (roughly 6 feet, 2 inches, or 1.88 meters)," citing *Ietada Nikki* but providing no additional verification of the source material.
- In the same year, *University of King's College* in Canada published an article describing Yasuke with the same height, also citing this misinterpretation without reviewing the original Japanese text.

Thus, by the end of 2019, the incorrect height of 188 cm was well-established in the public and academic narrative. This marked a classic case of circular reporting, where one misinterpreted figure on Wikipedia was repeated by major institutions and publications.

FURTHER COMPOUNDING THE MYTH: REPEATED MISQUOTES AND THE ROLE OF WIKIPEDIA

By 2023, Wikipedia had become a central node in the dissemination of the false information. In the 2013 version of the Yasuke article, his height is listed as 188 cm (6 shaku 2 sun. This false information formed the backbone of multiple reports across platforms.

For instance:

- *Britannica* and *University of King's College* both relied on Wikipedia's error, repeating the same measurements and descriptions without cross-referencing with the original Japanese texts.
- The website *yasuke-san.com* mirrored the Wikipedia entry, providing further validation to the circular nature of this reporting. The repetition of the same wording and measurements across sources created a veneer of credibility, even though the claims were never verified.

A CHANGE IN WIKIPEDIA AND CIRCULAR REPORTING IN ACTION

In 2017, the Wikipedia article on Yasuke was updated again, this time refining some of the language but maintaining the same basic errors. By this point, the mistranslation of "sumi" to "charcoal" had become embedded in the narrative, and Yasuke's height remained inflated to 188 cm.

Even as corrections were made in some sources by 2024, such as *Britannica* revising its article to remove certain claims about Yasuke's height and appearance, the myth persisted elsewhere. The circular reporting had already done its damage: countless articles, blog posts, and even scholarly papers were now citing the false information that originated from the unverified Wikipedia entry.

THE POWER OF CIRCULAR REPORTING

The story of Yasuke is a textbook case of circular reporting. An initial misinterpretation on Wikipedia about Yasuke's height and appearance became the foundation for articles by prestigious media outlets like the *BBC* and *Britannica*, as well as academic institutions. The lack of proper source verification allowed these errors to spread unchecked, with each new article reinforcing the credibility of the last. The mistranslations and misinterpretations, particularly around Yasuke's height and skin color, became accepted facts through constant repetition.

The consequences of this circular reporting are clear: the historical Yasuke has been overshadowed by a mythologized version, where inaccuracies about his height and skin color have taken root in public consciousness. Only by returning to the original sources, such as *Ietada Nikki*, and conducting proper fact-checking can these myths be unraveled.

YASUKE AS A LORD: CROWD SPECULATION, NOT NOBUNAGA'S PLAN

The rumor that Yasuke was going to be made a lord (*tono*) by Oda Nobunaga is widely repeated today. However, this notion stems from a misunderstanding of historical records, where speculation by onlookers was mistaken for actual plans. The original report by Jesuit priest Lorenzo Mesia, often cited in these discussions, is the source of this misunderstanding.

THE ORIGINAL PHRASE AND ITS MEANING

The core phrase in question comes from Mesia's report, written in 1581:

Original Portuguese: *Dizem que o fará Tono.*

This phrase has been interpreted as meaning "They say he will make him a lord." But let's break this down to understand its actual meaning and context.

- Dizem: "They say" or "it is said."
- que: "That."
- o: "Him."
- fará: "Will make" (from *fazer*).
- Tono: The Japanese title for "lord" or *tono* (殿).

A direct translation is: "They say he will make him a lord."

At first glance, this seems straightforward. However, the critical point here is who is doing the saying. The phrase "they say" (*dizem que*) signals that this is not a statement from Nobunaga or any official figure, but rather what other people were saying, likely based on observations or assumptions. In other words, this was a rumor—a speculative comment from onlookers, not a plan or decision made by Nobunaga himself.

THE CONTEXT OF THE STATEMENT

To understand why this speculation arose, it's important to look at the events surrounding this phrase. Mesia's report describes how Nobunaga was impressed with Yasuke, pleased with his presence, and had him paraded around the city. Nobunaga assigned one of his close attendants to escort Yasuke through the streets, which was an unusual display. The original text of Mesia's report states:

"Nobunaga liked him very much and favored him so much that he sent him around the city with one of his close attendants, so that everyone would know he was favored. They say he will make him a lord (tono)."

In this context, the speculation that Yasuke might become a lord arose not from Nobunaga's own words or actions but from the spectacle of Yasuke being paraded with Nobunaga's personal attendant. Seeing this unusual situation, onlookers may have jumped to conclusions, interpreting it as a sign that Yasuke was being elevated to a higher status.

NO OFFICIAL PLAN FROM NOBUNAGA

The key point is that this rumor came from the crowd observing Yasuke, not from any declaration or intention by Nobunaga. In fact, there is no record of Nobunaga ever stating or indicating that Yasuke would be made a lord. The original Portuguese phrase *dizem que*—"they say"—is crucial here, as it reflects gossip or speculation by bystanders, rather than an official plan.

Furthermore, in the historical context of 16th-century Japan, becoming a lord (*tono*) was a significant event, usually involving military achievement, governance, or high-level service to the state. Yasuke, having only recently arrived in Japan and entered Nobunaga's service, would not have met the typical requirements for such an elevation. Nobunaga was known to reward merit and loyalty, but there is no documentation or credible evidence suggesting that Yasuke was being positioned for such a role.

TRANSLATION ERRORS EXAGGERATED THE SPECULATION

The misunderstanding likely worsened due to translation issues. When translated into Japanese, the original Portuguese future tense (*fará*, meaning "will do") was sometimes overemphasized, leading to phrases like "将来" (shōrai, meaning "in the future") or "ゆくゆくは" (yukuyuku wa, meaning "eventually"). These additions gave the false impression that Nobunaga had long-term plans for Yasuke to become a lord, when in fact, Mesia's report only reflects passing speculation.

As this misinterpretation spread, the phrase became distorted into claims that Nobunaga had actual "plans" to make Yasuke a *tono* or even "one day rule a castle." These exaggerations moved far beyond the original statement, which only reflected rumors circulating among onlookers.

THE ROLE OF NOBUNAGA'S ATTENDANTS

One of the reasons this rumor started is the fact that Yasuke was escorted through the city by one of Nobunaga's personal attendants, which gave the appearance of high status. The original phrase in Mesia's report describes the attendant as someone very close to Nobunaga, emphasizing how unusual this display was.

In the original Portuguese, the text reads: *"mandou por toda a cidade com hem homem seu muito privado,"* meaning Nobunaga sent Yasuke around the city with "a very private man of his" (one of his close personal attendants).[86] This action likely made Yasuke appear to be a person of great importance, which could have led people to speculate that he was being treated as a lord.

However, this was an interpretation by the crowd, not something stated by Nobunaga. The act of parading Yasuke through the city was likely more about showing off Nobunaga's exotic and impressive retainer, rather than signaling any official intention to make him a lord.

THE ABSENCE OF CONCRETE PLANS

When we look at other historical records, such as the *Ietada Nikki* (『家忠日記』) or the *Shinchō Kōki* (『信長公記』), there is no mention of any formal plans to elevate Yasuke to a noble title or make him a lord. If Nobunaga had truly intended to grant Yasuke such a status, it would have been noted in these significant historical texts.

Furthermore, the notion of a foreigner being granted such a high position in 16th-century Japan would have been exceptional and therefore would have been recorded in more detail if it were true.

---

[86] This has often been exaggerated to say "'*his performance on the battlefield and patrol duties were recognized, leading him to rise to the core of the samurai ranks*" which is not present in the original text. (See Appendix)

The fact that it is absent from major chronicles suggests that it was nothing more than crowd speculation, not an official act.

The portrayal of Yasuke in historical texts, and the linguistic evolution surrounding how he was referenced, offers insight into how later alterations or misinterpretations may have shaped his legacy. A key example of this is seen in the difference between the terms "Kurobōzu" (黒坊主) and "Kurobō" (黒坊), both used to describe black-skinned individuals in Japanese records.

LOCKLEY'S SELECTION OF VISUAL SOURCES AND THEIR IMPLICATIONS

Thomas Lockley, in his work *Nobunaga to Yasuke* (信長と弥助), references visual sources such as the *Nanban Byōbu* (南蛮屏風, "Southern Barbarians Screens") to suggest Yasuke's role as a bodyguard. However, his reliance on lesser-known artworks, like those from the Amsterdam Museum, raises questions. These pieces, dating back to the 1610s, depict Portuguese and Spanish visitors, often accompanied by black servants, and are part of a larger collection of similar works that followed earlier prototypes.

Lockley emphasizes certain visual cues, such as a black man holding a spear, to suggest Yasuke's role as a warrior. However, in other more prominent works, such as those from the Nagasaki History and Culture Museum, this same figure holds a flag, not a weapon. Lockley's choice to use more obscure pieces like those from the Amsterdam Museum seems intentional, as these depictions could more easily be interpreted in line with his thesis of Yasuke being a "bodyguard"—a role requiring weaponry. In contrast, other, better-known *Nanban Byōbu*, like those from the Kanō school, show black figures without weapons, complicating such interpretations.

THE LINGUISTIC EVOLUTION OF "KUROBŌZU" VS. "KUROBŌ"

A key linguistic shift that reveals much about the evolution of Yasuke's depiction lies in the terminology used to describe him. In earlier records, like the *Shinchō Kōki* (信長公記), Yasuke is referred to as "Kurobōzu" (黒坊主), a term literally meaning "black monk" but often used to describe a black man, with the suffix "bōzu" indicating a Buddhist monk or bald man. In other contemporary accounts, such as the *Ietada Nikki* (家忠日記), Yasuke is referred to as "Kuro-otoko" (くろ男), meaning "black man."

However, in later texts like the *Sonkeikaku version* of the *Shinchō Kōki*, Yasuke is called "Kurobō" (黒坊), dropping the "zu" and using a more simplified term. This subtle shift in language is not trivial. The term "Kurobō" appears to be a later innovation, reflecting a linguistic evolution that may have occurred as the term became more generalized over time, referring less specifically to Yasuke's status as a monk or servant and more broadly to a black individual.

This shift suggests that later copyists, operating during periods when the term "Kurobō" had become more standardized, altered the original text to reflect contemporary language. In this sense, the change from "Kurobōzu" to "Kurobō" indicates that the version of the *Shinchō Kōki* in which this appears is likely a later revision, reflecting the broader societal usage of "Kurobō."

TEXTUAL ALTERATIONS AND THEIR IMPLICATIONS

The implication of this linguistic change is significant. If the *Sonkeikaku* version of the *Shinchō Kōki*, which references Yasuke as "Kurobō," was indeed altered, it means that descriptions of Yasuke were subject to reinterpretation long after the events in question. This opens the possibility that the Yasuke described in this version is not identical to the Yasuke described by contemporary sources.

Lockley's reliance on these later texts and visual interpretations can thus be problematic. His selection of sources that reflect a more mythologized and generalized view of black men in Japan (through the use of "Kurobō") may contribute to a distortion of Yasuke's actual historical role. Instead of relying on earlier records where the term "Kurobōzu" clearly denotes Yasuke's identity as a black man who was likely a servant or monk, the later term "Kurobō" introduces ambiguity about his status.

THE IMPORTANCE OF TERMINOLOGY IN HISTORICAL INTERPRETATION

The linguistic shift from "Kurobōzu" to "Kurobō" is not merely a technicality—it reflects a broader change in how black figures like Yasuke were perceived and remembered in Japanese culture. Lockley's interpretations, which selectively use visual and textual sources that align with a more heroic, bodyguard-like portrayal of Yasuke, may inadvertently contribute to a mythologization that ignores these crucial linguistic and historical distinctions.

In *African Samurai*, Lockley and Girard make a statement that *Ōta Gyūichi's* biography, *The Chronicle of Nobunaga*, was published posthumously, about ten years after Ōta's death, and that it was printed using a movable type printing press. This particular claim, however, raises significant issues regarding the source material they reference, as it appears that they are confusing two different works: *Ōta Gyūichi's Shinchō Kōki* (信長公記) and *Ōse Bōan's* (小瀬甫庵) later *Bōan Shinchōki* (甫庵信長記).

MOVABLE TYPE AND ITS IMPLICATIONS

The movable type printing press was indeed a notable technological advancement that made a resurgence in the early 17th century, but this method of printing was not used for *Ōta Gyūichi's Shinchō Kōki*, the original chronicle of Nobunaga. The *Shinchō Kōki* was originally written as a manuscript, circulating in handwritten form during Gyūichi's lifetime and shortly after his death. The confusion arises from the fact that movable type was used in the printing of *Ōse Bōan's Bōan Shinchōki*, a later work that was published in 1622, nearly a decade after *Ōta Gyūichi's* death.

The *Bōan Shinchōki*, while based on *Ōta's* work, includes significant embellishments and creative liberties, making it less reliable as a historical source compared to *Ōta's* more factual and direct chronicle. The distinction between these two works is crucial because Lockley appears to reference *Ōse Bōan's* version, not *Ōta's* original text, when discussing *The Chronicle of Nobunaga* in *African Samurai*. This is evidenced by the mention of movable type printing, which did not apply to *Ōta's* original chronicle.

WHY THIS IS PROBLEMATIC

The confusion between *Ōta Gyūichi's* factual *Shinchō Kōki* and *Ōse Bōan's* embellished *Bōan Shinchōki* creates several problems in terms of historical accuracy:

1. Loss of Factual Integrity: *Ōse Bōan* introduced fictionalized accounts and dramatized events in *Bōan Shinchōki*. If Lockley used this version of the text as a reference, it could lead to the inclusion of historically inaccurate or exaggerated information in his portrayal of Yasuke. The original *Shinchō Kōki* is regarded as a more trustworthy record of events, particularly for matters like Nobunaga's life and his interactions with figures like Yasuke.

2. Yasuke's Presence in *Bōan Shinchōki* is Uncertain: There is no clear evidence that Yasuke (or his descriptions as "Kurobōzu") appears in the *Bōan Shinchōki*. If Lockley is drawing from this later, fictionalized account, it further diminishes the reliability of any reference to Yasuke's role or significance, as the embellishments in the *Bōan Shinchōki* could overshadow factual accounts from *Ōta's* original chronicle.

3. Historical Context: The fact that *Ōta's* work was a manuscript passed down in handwritten form adds weight to its historical value. Confusing this with a printed, more

widely distributed, and embellished version removes some of the contextual authenticity that comes with *Ōta's* first-hand account. *Ōta Gyūichi* was a direct witness to many of Nobunaga's activities, giving his chronicle a degree of accuracy that is not found in *Bōan's* later retelling.

We find further discrepancies in explinations concerning the *Honnō-ji* incident. The claim made in *African Samurai* that Yasuke fought alongside 30 men during the *Honnō-ji* incident, where Oda Nobunaga met his end, is historically incorrect. This claim significantly underreports the actual number of people who died with Nobunaga, as recorded in the most reliable historical source, *Shinchō Kōki* (信長公記).

According to *Shinchō Kōki,* which is considered the most factual account of Nobunaga's life and death, far more than 30 individuals perished during the Honnō-ji incident. The record lists:

- 4 people from Nobunaga's personal stables (御厩)
- 24 from the ranks of the middle-level attendants (御中間衆)
- 26 from within the palace grounds (御殿之内)

This gives a total of 54 people, not including Nobunaga himself, who died during the attack (he committed suicide). So, the idea that Yasuke was part of a group of only 30 is a significant misrepresentation of the actual number of people involved in the defense of Nobunaga.

WHY THIS DISCREPANCY?

Lockley, in his work, appears to rely on a mixture of sources, including Jesuit records and *Shinchō Kōki*, but he seems to have selectively omitted certain facts. It's likely that the count of 30 men is based on a selective reading of the sources, perhaps influenced by a desire to emphasize Yasuke's role. In reality, the total number of casualties was much higher than the 30 stated by Lockley, and the exclusion of lower-ranking attendants in the count suggests an attempt to elevate Yasuke's position in the event.

POSSIBLE MISINTERPRETATION

The inaccurate figure of 30 people might also stem from the narrative tendency to place Yasuke in a more prominent position, portraying him as one of Nobunaga's closest warriors, standing alongside him in his final moments. By ignoring the lower-ranking attendants who were also present and who fought bravely, Lockley's narrative positions Yasuke as one of a select few, which bolsters the idea that Yasuke held a prestigious role.

ROMANTICIZATION OF YASUKE'S ROLE

The way Yasuke's role is portrayed in *African Samurai* also fits into a common pattern of storytelling in which a non-native character is elevated above the locals. This narrative style, sometimes referred to as the "mighty whitey" or "black savior" trope, tends to place the outsider in a superior position to the indigenous people, often showing the outsider as being more skilled or closer to the leadership (in this case, Nobunaga) than the native population. In this version of the story, Yasuke is presented as having a special relationship with Nobunaga, while the contributions of lower-status Japanese retainers are downplayed or ignored.

By reducing the number of defenders to 30 and focusing on Yasuke's presence, Lockley's story aligns with a narrative where Yasuke is exceptional, possibly at the expense of historical accuracy. The real historical records, however, present a more complex and nuanced picture, where Yasuke was part of a much larger group of loyal retainers, many of whom died defending their lord at Honnō-ji.

The erroneous use of "カルサン弥助" (Karusan Yasuke) and the transformation into "Kurusan" is an example of how fiction and mistaken interpretations can inflate the historical significance of Yasuke.

CALÇÃO AND "KURUSAN YASUKE"

In Ryōu Kurusu's children's literature "くろ助" (Kurosuke),
Yasuke is given the nickname "カルサン弥助" (Karusan Yasuke),
based on the calção (Portuguese for trousers) worn by the
Portuguese depicted in the 南蛮屏風 (Namban byōbu), or
"Southern Barbarian Folding Screens." The name "Karusan"
comes from the Portuguese word for trousers, and in the context of
the story, this seems to serve as a playful or creative way of giving
Yasuke a more "samurai-like" name, as "Yasuke" by itself may
have sounded too informal to fit the typical naming conventions of
samurai at the time and as we have seen, all samurai had surnames.

In the fictional account, Yasuke is also sometimes referred to as "
カルサンどの" (Karusan-dono), using the honorific title "dono" to
further enhance the idea of his being elevated or treated with
respect, suggesting a noble status that wasn't historically accurate.

MISINTERPRETATION IN WESTERN SOURCES: "KURUSAN YASUKE"

What complicates the matter further is how this fictional name was
later misrepresented in English and French sources. The English
translation of the children's book introduced "Kurusan Yasuke,"
mixing the original "Karusan" with a misunderstanding of the
Japanese word "kuro" (黒), meaning black. The name "Kurusan"

was derived from this incorrect assumption, where "kuru" (coming from "kuro") was supposed to reference Yasuke's dark skin, which was historically mentioned. The addition of the honorific "-san" creates the illusion of formality, but in a somewhat awkward and anachronistic way.

This error was perpetuated in early versions of both English and French Wikipedia, where Yasuke was sometimes referred to as "Kuru-san," implying that this was a historical or meaningful designation. In the French version, this misinformation remained uncorrected for over a decade, with the name "Kuru-san" even making its way into popular culture, including a comic titled "Kurusan, le samouraï noir" (Kurusan, the Black Samurai).

INFLATING YASUKE'S IMPORTANCE

The use of "Kurusan" and similar titles gives the misleading impression that Yasuke held a formal position as a samurai with a full name or title, when in reality, Yasuke did not have a Japanese surname, nor was he a samurai. Samurai status in Japan came with clear markers, including a clan name, a fiefdom, and often a detailed genealogy, none of which Yasuke had. His name, "Yasuke," was a given or simplified name and not part of a formal samurai title.

The adaptation of his name to "Kurusan" in Western sources seems to be an attempt to give him a more formal or romanticized identity, turning him into a figure with a title and thus inflating his historical role.

The portrayal of Yasuke in *African Samurai*, particularly regarding the "Daikokuten theory," illustrates a troubling trend of deification and an Orientalist approach to interpreting his story. The book imposes a romanticized and exaggerated view of both Yasuke and Japanese culture, distorting the historical figure's role and the way he was actually perceived.

DEIFICATION OF YASUKE AS DAIKOKUTEN (大黒天)

Lockley asserts in *African Samurai* that Japanese people seem to have had no negative images associated with dark skin at this period in history and even revered it due to depictions of the Buddha and Daikokuten (大黒天), the Japanese version of the Indian god Shiva, who is often portrayed with dark, ebony-black skin[87]. This notion claims that Japanese admiration for Yasuke stemmed from an association with the revered black-skinned deity. While intriguing, this claim is problematic on several levels.

---

[87] Lockley, T., & Girard, G. (2019). *African samurai: The true story of Yasuke, a legendary black warrior in feudal Japan*. Hanover Square Press. p. 106-107

First, the connection between Yasuke and Daikokuten (大黒天) is speculative and lacks historical basis. The deification of Yasuke through this lens reflects an attempt to exalt him into something more than he was—a glorification common in Orientalist narratives. Japanese records, such as *Nobunaga no Yabōki* (信長公記) by Ōta Gyūichi (太田牛一), do not contain any mention of such reverence, let alone comparisons to deities like Daikokuten. Instead, Yasuke was simply referred to as a "Kurobōzu" (黒坊主), or "black monk," which reflects the cultural perception of his unusual appearance, rather than divine admiration.

THE PEOPLE OF KYOTO AND THE "LIVING DAIKOKUTEN"

Another point raised in *African Samurai* involves a scene where the people of Kyoto (京都) are said to have become "overcome with excitement" upon seeing Yasuke, even tearing at his clothes and scratching his skin, as if seeking a "souvenir" from their encounter with the "real live Daikokuten—the black god of prosperity".[88] This description not only deifies Yasuke but also frames the Japanese people in an almost primitive, fetishizing light, as if they were engaging in some kind of "trophy hunting" behavior. The use of terms like "gnarled peasant nails" adds a layer

---

[88] p. 113

198

of condescension toward the Japanese, as if portraying them as uncivilized or overly superstitious.

Such interpretations bear a disturbing similarity to Orientalist narratives that depict "the East" as exotic, backward, and overly mystical. The implication that Yasuke's dark skin alone would cause such a reaction from the Japanese reflects a skewed view, one that ignores the historical and cultural complexity of Japan during the Sengoku (戦国) period. Yasuke's uniqueness was certainly noted, but there is no reliable evidence that suggests he was viewed as anything divine or god-like.

THE MISINTERPRETATION OF NOBUNAGA'S REACTION

Lockley also suggests that when Nobunaga (信長) first encountered Yasuke, he associated him with Daikokuten, stating, "Black was the color—if one believed in such things—of gods and demons, not men"[89]. However, this interpretation is contradicted by primary Japanese sources, such as *Shinchō Kōki* (信長公記), where Nobunaga is recorded to have compared Yasuke to an ox, stating his skin was "black like an ox" (黒き事牛の如く). This comparison lacks the divine connotations that Lockley tries to introduce. The emphasis on blackness as being tied to "gods and

---

[89] p. 140

demons" appears more as a Western projection onto Japanese culture, fitting the narrative of Yasuke as an exotic figure.

VISUAL MISREPRESENTATIONS: THE CASE OF KIYOMIZU TEMPLE (清水寺)

Lockley further claims that Nobunaga had seen depictions of Daikokuten (大黒天) at Kiyomizu Temple (清水寺), suggesting that Yasuke's appearance triggered these associations. However, historically, the Daikokuten statue at Kiyomizu Temple would not have been located where Lockley implies during Nobunaga's lifetime. The current structure at the temple was rebuilt after 1633, well after Nobunaga's death in 1582. Additionally, the Daikokuten images from this period did not focus on black skin, as Lockley suggests, but rather depicted a plump, jolly figure, typically holding a sack and mallet—far removed from any resemblance to Yasuke. These historical inconsistencies suggest that Lockley may have been using selective information to support the narrative of Yasuke's near-divine status.

HOW HISTORY BECAME FICTION

The perception of Yasuke as a full-fledged samurai is largely a product of modern romanticization and has been heavily influenced by his depiction in anime, manga, and video games. While Yasuke certainly held a minor position in Nobunaga's household, historical evidence suggests that he likely served as a koshō (小姓), or personal attendant, rather than being officially elevated to full samurai status. The portrayal of Yasuke as a samurai in popular media has shaped how he is understood today, often obscuring the historical realities of his life and role in Japan. Further, Afrocentrist activists have used this account as a way of supporting unhistorical events in Europe and Asia.[90]

ROMANTICIZATION OF YASUKE IN POPULAR CULTURE

In recent years, Yasuke's story has been embraced by various forms of Japanese media, where he is frequently depicted as a samurai and sometimes even as a legendary figure who played a major role in Nobunaga's campaigns. These portrayals reflect a

---

[90] Rashidi, R. (2011). *Black star: The African presence in early Europe*. Books of Africa.

romanticized vision of Yasuke's life, casting him as a heroic, skilled warrior and a fully recognized member of the samurai class. This reimagining appeals to contemporary audiences who are fascinated by the idea of a foreigner—particularly an African man—ascending to such a respected and elite position in feudal Japan.

EXAMPLES IN ANIME, MANGA, AND VIDEO GAMES

1. YASUKE (弥助, 2021)

Anime: Yasuke (弥助) is a Netflix original anime released in 2021. This series is the most direct and well-known depiction of Yasuke, portraying him as a legendary Black samurai. While the historical Yasuke likely served as a retainer and attendant to Oda Nobunaga, this anime presents him as a full-fledged samurai, deeply involved in key events and battles, often using fantasy elements like magic and mechs. The show blends history with fiction, showing Yasuke fighting not only political and military foes but also supernatural enemies.

- Studio: MAPPA
- Director: LeSean Thomas

2. AFRO SAMURAI (アフロサムライ)

Anime and Manga: Afro Samurai (アフロサムライ), while not directly about Yasuke, features a Black samurai protagonist who roams a feudal Japan-inspired world seeking revenge. This iconic series portrays the Afrocentric warrior as a master swordsman, blending Japanese samurai culture with a Black hero, drawing loose inspiration from historical figures like Yasuke. Afro Samurai plays a key role in popularizing the idea of a Black samurai, helping solidify the image of Yasuke as a powerful, mythical warrior in Japanese and global popular culture.

- Creator: Takashi Okazaki (岡崎能士)
- Studio: Gonzo

3. NIOH (仁王, 2017)

Video Game: Nioh, an action RPG set during the Sengoku period, features a fictionalized version of Yasuke as a formidable warrior. In the game, Yasuke serves Oda Nobunaga and is portrayed as a skilled fighter who assists the player character in various missions. The game blends historical elements with fantasy and supernatural themes, much like many other depictions of Yasuke, emphasizing his role as a samurai despite the lack of historical evidence supporting his full integration into the samurai class.

- Developer: Team Ninja

4. SHUUMATSU NO WALKÜRE (終末のワルキューレ, RECORD OF RAGNAROK)

Manga: While Yasuke hasn't appeared as a main character yet, there is ongoing speculation in the fan community that he may be featured in future arcs of Shuumatsu no Walküre (Record of Ragnarok), a manga where historical and mythological figures from different cultures battle against gods. Given that Oda Nobunaga is a prominent character in the series, Yasuke is often mentioned as a potential future addition. The legendary warrior status of Yasuke continues to grow in speculative works like this, contributing to the broader mythologization of him as a samurai.

- Authors: Shinya Umemura (梅村真也), Takumi Fukui (フクイタクミ)
- Artist: Ajichika (アジチカ)

WHY YASUKE IS VIEWED AS A SAMURAI

The idea of Yasuke as a samurai has gained widespread traction due to several factors:

Cultural Fascination with the Samurai Class: The samurai are often seen as symbols of honor, skill, and martial prowess, and the idea of a foreigner—particularly a man of African descent—joining their ranks appeals to modern sensibilities. Yasuke's story has been reinterpreted to fit this narrative, often glossing over the more nuanced historical realities of his role as a retainer.

Representation and Symbolism: The story of Yasuke, particularly when framed as one of a foreigner achieving elite warrior status in a foreign land, resonates with modern audiences seeking more diverse historical narratives. This has led to Yasuke being portrayed as a symbol of racial achievement and integration in popular media, which in turn reinforces the idea of him being a full samurai.

Historical Ambiguity: The lack of detailed historical records about Yasuke's life allows for artistic interpretation and exaggeration. Since the exact details of his role under Nobunaga are sparse, creators of anime, manga, and games have had the freedom to fill in the gaps, often by transforming Yasuke into a legendary figure who rises to the status of samurai.

Romanticism of Foreign Influence: Yasuke's presence in Japan, especially as a foreigner in a position of trust within Nobunaga's household, has been romanticized. His story is often retold as one of an outsider who, through strength and loyalty, becomes part of the Japanese warrior elite. This idealized narrative has become more appealing to audiences than the historical reality of Yasuke's more limited role as a koshō or retainer.

Japanese media—particularly anime, manga, and video games—has played a significant role in the country's soft power strategy, aiming to spread Japanese culture and values across the globe. This cultural influence, known as Cool Japan, has been effective in making elements of Japanese history, customs, and aesthetics widely known and appreciated by foreign audiences. However, this approach can sometimes lead to unintended consequences, particularly when it comes to the historic accuracy of events and figures. The romanticized, fictionalized depictions of Japanese history, such as the portrayal of samurai or figures like Yasuke, can blur the line between historical fact and fiction for foreign audiences who may have limited access to accurate sources.

EXPANSION OF JAPANESE CULTURE THROUGH MEDIA

Japan's media industry, especially its anime, manga, and video games, has become a global phenomenon, shaping how millions of people around the world perceive Japanese culture. These forms of entertainment often incorporate elements of Japanese history, mythology, and samurai culture, but they are typically crafted with an emphasis on entertainment rather than historical accuracy. This blending of fantasy and history makes Japanese media accessible and appealing to a wide audience, expanding Japan's cultural influence and soft power across the globe.

For example, in stories such as Yasuke (弥助) and Afro Samurai (アフロサムライ), figures from Japan's feudal past are often reimagined and stylized for narrative purposes, which can make these works more engaging for viewers. These media products promote a sense of cultural intrigue and admiration for samurai ideals, but they often obscure or distort the true historical context behind these figures, resulting in fictitious stereotypes.

DAMAGING HISTORICAL ACCURACY

While the success of Japan's soft power strategy through media is undeniable, the historicity of Japanese events and figures can suffer when fiction is prioritized over fact. For many non-Japanese audiences, especially Westerners, the lines between historical events and fictional narratives can easily blur. This is compounded by the fact that many foreigners have limited access to reliable sources or accurate Japanese-language materials that could clarify the historical truths behind the popularized figures they see in anime and manga.

Several key factors contribute to this problem:

1. Limited Access to Accurate Historical Sources: Many foreign audiences rely heavily on translated works or media intended for entertainment, which may not offer accurate depictions of historical events. Additionally, primary Japanese historical texts or academic research on figures like Yasuke may not be available or easily accessible in foreign languages, further restricting the ability of Western audiences to get an accurate picture.

2. Romanticization of Figures Like Yasuke: In works like the Yasuke anime or Afro Samurai, the romanticization of Yasuke as a full-fledged samurai plays into the foreign fascination with samurai culture but departs significantly from the historical reality, which is more nuanced and limited. Yasuke's likely role as a koshō (小姓) or retainer, without full samurai status, is overshadowed by the more attractive narrative of him being a legendary warrior in Japanese media. For those without access to historical records, these depictions become the accepted truth.

3. Fictionalization of Japanese History in Popular Media: Many Japanese media products blend history and fantasy seamlessly, making it difficult for foreign audiences to distinguish between fact and fiction. For example, games like Nioh and series like Drifters (ドリフターズ), which feature historical figures in fantastical settings, do not explicitly signal which elements are historically accurate

and which are fictional. This creates a narrow and skewed vision of Japanese history for audiences who take these portrayals at face value.

4. Western Misunderstanding of Japanese Fiction: Many Western audiences are unfamiliar with the depth and complexity of Japanese storytelling and its long tradition of blending historical elements with myth and legend. As a result, they may mistake these fictionalized accounts for actual historical events, failing to recognize that what they are seeing is often entertainment, not education.

PROPAGATION OF FICTITIOUS STEREOTYPES

The tendency for Japanese media to romanticize and embellish historical figures—especially ones that involve samurai culture or figures like Yasuke—can lead to the propagation of stereotypes. For example, many Westerners now associate Yasuke primarily with the samurai class, despite historical evidence suggesting his role was more limited. This inaccurate representation can spread easily, especially in a world where online content and social media play a large role in shaping cultural perceptions.

Furthermore, the lack of nuanced portrayals of Japanese history in globally popular media reinforces stereotypical images of Japan as a land of warriors, samurai, and exotic foreigners like Yasuke, rather than offering a more realistic understanding of Japan's complex history and social hierarchy.

The misunderstanding of Japanese culture and history has been further exacerbated by some factions within the Afrocentrist movement. While Afrocentrism initially aimed to reclaim African history from Eurocentric narratives, certain extreme offshoots of the movement have made bold and unsupported claims about African influence on other world cultures[91],[92], including Japan. One of the more notable and modern claims put forward by Afrocentrist figures is that Japanese culture, particularly samurai culture, was influenced or even started by Africans.

A prominent figure in this movement, Umar Johnson, has even gone as far as to claim that "to be a samurai, you must have Black blood." This claim has no historical basis in Japan, and it reflects the extreme fringes of Afrocentrism, which distort history for their own aims. Johnson's assertion, and others like it, represents a misunderstanding of both Japanese history and Japanese language, relying on modern interpretations and anachronistic ideas rather than genuine historical evidence.

---

[91] Runoko Rashidi, Ivan Van Sertima (1988) African Presence in Early Asia, Journal of African civilizations, ISSN 0270-2495

[92] De Graft-Johnson, J. C. (1937). *African glory: The story of vanished Negro civilizations*. Watts & Co.

ORIGIN OF THE CLAIM

Umar Johnson, a controversial figure known for his Afrocentric rhetoric, has been cited making the claim that "to be a samurai, you must have Black blood." The origins of this statement are entirely modern and non-Japanese. This idea likely stems from the romanticized portrayal of figures like Yasuke, the African man who served Oda Nobunaga, who is sometimes falsely depicted as a full-fledged samurai in media. However, there is no historical evidence, in Japanese or otherwise, to support the claim that samurai status was contingent on African ancestry or any Black lineage.

The idea that Japanese culture, particularly its warrior class, was influenced by or connected to Africans is a narrative that has been pushed by some Afrocentrists who aim to position African peoples as the originators of many world cultures. However, the historical development of samurai culture is well-documented in Japan, and it is clear that it evolved independently from African influences.

NO BASIS IN JAPANESE SOURCES

It is important to emphasize that no original Japanese historical texts or credible academic sources support the claim that "to be a samurai, you must have Black blood." This phrase does not appear in Japanese-language sources, and the idea that samurai had to be of African descent is a modern fabrication with no historical roots. The notion that samurai required "Black blood" is a misrepresentation, most likely born out of the desire to connect Africa to the samurai tradition, rather than any actual historical fact.

THE MISUNDERSTANDING OF "BLACK BLOOD" IN JAPANESE CONTEXT

Adding to the confusion, if the phrase "Black blood" were to exist in a Japanese cultural or linguistic context, it would have an entirely different meaning from what Afrocentrists claim. In Japanese idiomatic expressions, "Black blood" (黒い血, *kuroi chi*) or references to blackness are sometimes used metaphorically to describe a person's ruthlessness, merciless nature, or cold-blooded behavior. This usage has no connection to race or ethnicity, and it certainly doesn't imply African descent.

For instance, in Japanese, to say someone has "Black blood" metaphorically could mean they have a dark, merciless nature or that they are willing to act in a cutthroat or brutal manner. It is a figurative expression unrelated to race, and even if such a saying existed in the context of samurai, it would likely refer to a warrior's willingness to show no mercy in battle, not to any racial or ethnic background.

Thus, even if the phrase "to be a samurai, you must have Black blood" were to exist in a Japanese context, it would not carry the racial connotations attributed to it by Afrocentrists. The Japanese concept of "Black blood" would be understood metaphorically as a trait describing a person's character or temperament, rather than their ancestry.

DISTORTING HISTORY FOR IDEOLOGICAL AIMS

The claim made by Umar Johnson, and similar assertions by others in the extreme Afrocentrist movement, reflects a broader trend of distorting history to fit ideological aims. While it is important to acknowledge the influences and contributions of African cultures to world history, claims like these—without evidence—ultimately do more harm than good. They create false narratives that detract from the real achievements and unique cultural developments of both Africa and Japan.

By inserting unsubstantiated claims into the historical record, these movements not only misrepresent Japanese culture but also obscure the true history of African influence on the world, which is already rich and diverse. Furthermore, these claims contribute to the misunderstanding of Japan's feudal period, creating fictitious stereotypes that foreign audiences are already prone to accept due to their limited access to Japanese-language sources.

The previously analyzed book "African Samurai: The True Story of Yasuke, a Legendary Black Warrior in Feudal Japan" by Geoffrey Girard and Thomas Lockley has played a significant role in shaping the modern Western understanding of Yasuke. The book has been widely promoted as a historical account of Yasuke's life and his role in feudal Japan, but it contains numerous embellishments and, in some cases, outright fabrications that distort both Yasuke's personal story and Japanese history. Although the book helped introduce Yasuke to a larger audience, it has unfortunately contributed to misconceptions about his true role and status, particularly the idea that he was a full samurai, an assertion not supported by historical evidence.

IMPACT OF THE BOOK ON YASUKE'S IMAGE IN THE WEST

Since its release, "African Samurai" has been influential in popularizing Yasuke's story in the West, portraying him as a full-fledged samurai who participated in the most critical moments of Oda Nobunaga's reign. This portrayal has captivated Western readers, intrigued by the idea of an African warrior rising to prominence in Japan. However, much of this narrative is either highly exaggerated or fabricated. The book draws from a romanticized and fictionalized version of Yasuke's life, relying on minimal historical documentation and filling in the gaps with speculative and imaginative details.

For example:

The idea that Yasuke was elevated to samurai status and wielded the katana (刀) as a full member of the bushi (武士) class lacks substantiated historical evidence. Ysuke's exact role was likely that of a retainer or koshō (小姓), acting as an attendant rather than a full warrior.

Speculative details about his personal interactions with other samurai or his participation in key battles are embellished without concrete sources to back them up. The romanticizing of Yasuke's life overshadows the more complex reality of what it meant to be a foreigner in Japan's strict social hierarchy.

INFLUENCE ON ASSASSIN'S CREED AND FURTHER DISTORTIONS

The portrayal of Yasuke in popular media further deviated from historical accuracy when the book by Girard and Lockley became a source of inspiration for Assassin's Creed: Shadows by . The Assassin's Creed series is well-known for using historical settings and characters, blending real events with fiction. In the case of Yasuke, however, the game developers relied on the romanticized portrayal from "African Samurai," which has only added to the misunderstanding of Yasuke's true historical role.

Assassin's Creed games present themselves as having historical authenticity, and many players believe the depictions of historical figures and settings are accurate representations. In this case, the game portrays Yasuke as a full samurai, a myth born from modern reimaginations rather than the actual historical record. The game also makes several basic historical errors regarding Japan itself, further complicating the player's understanding of Japanese history.

Examples of these inaccuracies include:

Seasonal Mistakes: The game features persimmons (kaki, 柿) on trees at the same time as sakura (桜) blossoms, which would not happen in reality. In Japan, sakura blooms in spring, while persimmons typically ripen in late autumn. This error shows a lack of attention to seasonal cycles, which are important in Japanese culture and aesthetics.

Misrepresented Architecture: Some of the architectural elements and items depicted in the game, rather than being authentically Japanese, are actually Chinese in origin. While Chinese influence on Japan was significant, especially during earlier periods like the Tang Dynasty, by the Azuchi-Momoyama period (安土桃山時代), Japan had developed its own distinctive styles. The game conflates Chinese and Japanese architecture, contributing to a misunderstanding of both cultures.

Ubisoft's portrayal of Yasuke wearing armor is not only historically inaccurate but also highly problematic. The armor depicted in their media is a strange combination of pieces from two distinct periods of Japanese history: the Kamakura period (鎌倉時

代, Kamakura-jidai) (1185–1333) and the Sengoku period (戦国時代, Sengoku-jidai) (1467–1615). This mixture of armors from different eras is not only incorrect but laughable when considering Yasuke's actual position and resources at the time.

Kamakura period armor, particularly the ō-yoroi (大鎧), was worn only by the highest-ranking samurai (侍), primarily those mounted on horseback. This type of armor was known for its elaborate design, including large shoulder guards (sode, 袖) and a heavy boxy structure, making it a symbol of prestige. By contrast, during the Sengoku period, armor had evolved to suit the needs of foot soldiers and large-scale warfare, favoring lighter, more practical designs such as the tosei gusoku (当世具足).

The idea of combining these two types of armor in one suit, as Ubisoft does, is entirely out of place. Kamakura period armor was no longer in fashion by the time Yasuke served Oda Nobunaga (織田信長), and Sengoku-era retainers typically wore more streamlined armor designed for mobility and effectiveness in battle.

Moreover, such high-ranking armor was incredibly expensive during both periods. A suit of ō-yoroi could cost the equivalent of several estates' worth of wealth in the Kamakura period, and modern estimates suggest that an authentic reproduction would cost tens of thousands, if not hundreds of thousands, of dollars today. For comparison, even the standard tosei gusoku from the Sengoku period, though simpler, would still be a significant investment.

It is highly improbable that Yasuke, a foreign retainer with a limited role, would be able to afford such prestigious armor. More importantly, it is equally unlikely that Nobunaga (信長) would permit a servant of Yasuke's rank to wear something so symbolically powerful, as armor of this caliber was reserved for high-ranking samurai or daimyō (大名). Yasuke, whose primary role was likely as a sword-bearer and bodyguard, would not have had the status or resources to don such an extravagant and historically misplaced suit of armor.

By presenting Yasuke in such armor, Ubisoft ignores the social and historical realities of the time, creating an image that is not only anachronistic but also misrepresents the actual hierarchy and limitations that Yasuke, as a retainer, would have faced. This portrayal feeds into modern myths about Yasuke's status while disregarding the detailed and strict social order of the Sengoku period.

These inaccuracies, combined with the distorted portrayal of Yasuke, demonstrate how Western media sometimes relies on surface-level interpretations of Japanese culture, missing out on the nuances and complexities that define its historical and cultural landscape.

THE PROBLEM OF HISTORICAL FICTION MASQUERADING AS FACT

One of the key issues with both Girard and Lockley's book and Assassin's Creed's portrayal of Yasuke is that they present speculative fiction as if it were historical fact. For many audiences, especially those unfamiliar with Japanese history, these depictions become the accepted narrative, blurring the line between fiction and reality. While fiction and entertainment can be effective tools for introducing historical figures like Yasuke to new audiences, the responsibility lies in ensuring that basic facts are not distorted for the sake of narrative appeal.

This distortion is problematic for a few reasons:

Misinformation: Readers and gamers may walk away with a misinformed understanding of Japanese history, especially regarding the samurai class and the strict social hierarchies of the time.

Cultural Misrepresentation: By relying on fictionalized accounts like "African Samurai," popular media risks misrepresenting both Yasuke's true role and broader aspects of Japanese culture. This can lead to the propagation of stereotypes and fictitious narratives, such as the idea that a foreigner could easily become a samurai, which was highly unlikely within the rigid class structure of feudal Japan.

Historical Integrity: The conflation of fact and fiction in historical portrayals weakens the historical integrity of both Yasuke's story and the Japanese period in which he lived. This not only affects scholarly discussions but also influences how future generations will understand Japan's past.

While the Afrocentrist movement and certain Western academics push their ideological narratives, they often overlook the glaring hypocrisy in their actions—particularly when it comes to appropriating Asian cultures. These same individuals and institutions are at the forefront of lecturing others on the supposed dangers of cultural appropriation, yet they themselves engage in it when it serves their agenda. At the same time, they champion Diversity, Equity, and Inclusion (DEI) as a guiding principle, but curiously, their commitment to cultural respect and historical accuracy seems to evaporate when it comes to Asian cultures. Social amnesia sets in, and the misrepresentation and appropriation of Japanese and other Asian histories are not only overlooked but sometimes actively encouraged.

HYPOCRISY IN CULTURAL APPROPRIATION AND DEI

The core tenet of cultural appropriation is the inappropriate adoption or use of elements from one culture by another, typically by a more dominant group, without understanding or respecting the original context. For years, Afrocentrist scholars, along with many Western academics aligned with DEI initiatives, have condemned the misuse or misrepresentation of African culture by non-Africans, arguing that it perpetuates stereotypes and leads to cultural erasure. Yet, when it comes to Japanese culture, particularly figures like Yasuke, they adopt a very different approach.

In pushing the narrative that Japanese culture, or the samurai class, was somehow influenced or even originated from Africa, they engage in the very cultural appropriation they claim to decry. Umar Johnson's claim that "to be a samurai, you must have Black blood" is a prime example of this hypocrisy. There is no historical or linguistic basis for such a statement, and it reflects a clear attempt to co-opt Japanese history for an Afrocentric agenda. Worse still, the phrase doesn't even originate in Japanese; it's an outright fabrication designed to promote an idea that has no roots in either Japanese history or culture.

SELECTIVE MEMORY AND SOCIAL AMNESIA IN DEI

The broader DEI movement, which emphasizes inclusion and cultural sensitivity, also falls into this pattern of selective outrage. In the rush to promote diversity and give voice to marginalized communities, there seems to be a collective forgetfulness when Asian cultures are being misrepresented or appropriated. The same individuals and groups who are vocal about the misappropriation of African or Indigenous cultures tend to go silent when Japanese history is reinterpreted or distorted to fit Western narratives.

Take, for example, media portrayals of Yasuke, where he is falsely depicted as a samurai in works like the book *"African Samurai"* and video games like Assassin's Creed: Shadows. This isn't just historical fiction—it's an intentional reimagining of Japanese history to fit a modern diversity agenda. The problem is not that Yasuke's story is being told, but that it's being rewritten in a way that strips it of historical accuracy, ultimately serving to promote an ideological narrative rather than historical truth.

When Western media companies like Netflix or Ubisoft—companies that champion DEI—produce content that distorts Japanese culture, the cultural integrity of Japan is erased, and the selective outrage of the DEI movement becomes glaring. Yet, there is little pushback, because the narrative of diversity and inclusion trumps the responsibility to honor the truth of another culture.

CULTURAL APPROPRIATION DISGUISED AS INCLUSION

Many of the same Afrocentrist figures and DEI advocates that distort Asian history in the name of "diversity" would likely be the first to decry any misrepresentation of their own cultures. Yet, when the roles are reversed, and it's Japanese history being rewritten to fit an Afrocentric or Western-centric narrative, they turn a blind eye. This creates a double standard that ultimately damages the integrity of both African and Asian cultures.

Take the claim by some Afrocentrists that Japanese culture was heavily influenced by Africa, or that African ancestry is a prerequisite for becoming a samurai. These claims not only have no historical backing, but they also serve to appropriate the unique cultural and social development of Japan for another agenda. If anyone made similarly unsubstantiated claims about African or Indigenous cultures, these same groups would be outraged, calling it erasure or colonization of their history.

CULTURAL APPRECIATION VS. APPROPRIATION

The issue at hand is not that different cultures should be separated or held apart—quite the opposite. Cultural appreciation involves engaging with and learning from other cultures with respect and humility. It's about celebrating diversity without rewriting history. Each culture has its own unique identity and history, and we can enjoy and celebrate them without feeling the need to force connections that don't exist.

The story of Yasuke is fascinating in its own right: a foreigner who became a trusted retainer in the household of Oda Nobunaga during a tumultuous period in Japanese history. His presence alone is a testimony to cultural interactions and unique historical moments. We can appreciate Yasuke's significance without needing to falsely elevate him to samurai status or invent claims about African influence on Japanese warrior culture.

By engaging in cultural appreciation rather than cultural appropriation, we can honor the true complexities of each culture. We can explore the rich traditions of Japanese history and African history without diminishing the integrity of either.

BATTLE OF HONNŌ-JI

The events leading up to Oda Nobunaga's (織田信長) betrayal and death at the Battle of Honnō-ji (本能寺の変) in 1582 are some of the most significant in Japanese history. Nobunaga, a powerful daimyō known for his ruthless tactics and ambition to unify Japan, was caught off guard by the betrayal of his trusted general, Akechi Mitsuhide (明智光秀). On June 21, 1582, Mitsuhide led a surprise attack against Nobunaga at Honnō-ji, the temple where Nobunaga was staying in Kyoto. Facing overwhelming odds and the certainty of capture, Nobunaga took his own life, a practice known as seppuku (切腹).

Yasuke (弥助), was present at the battle, serving as a retainer to Nobunaga. His documented role at Honnō-ji is one of the rare moments where he is directly mentioned in historical accounts. After Nobunaga's death, Yasuke was captured by Mitsuhide's forces. It's important to critically examine what the records say about Yasuke's actions during and after the battle, and how these differ from the sensationalized versions of his story.

THE BATTLE OF HONNŌ-JI AND YASUKE'S ROLE

Yasuke's role at Honnō-ji was that of a personal retainer and sword bearer for Nobunaga. Contrary to the popular narrative that casts him as a warrior fighting valiantly alongside Nobunaga, there is no evidence to suggest that Yasuke engaged in any significant combat. His role was likely one of protection and service, standing by his lord during the chaos of the attack. After Nobunaga committed seppuku, Yasuke did not display any of the behaviors traditionally associated with samurai honor. Instead of continuing the fight or dying alongside his master, Yasuke immediately gave himself up to Mitsuhide's forces.

YASUKE'S SURRENDER AND TREATMENT

One of the most telling aspects of Yasuke's capture is his swift surrender, which sharply contrasts with the idealized image of the samurai, who were expected to fight to the death or perform seppuku in such circumstances. This behavior strongly indicates that Yasuke was not viewed, nor did he see himself, as a true samurai.

According to Jesuit sources (イエズス会年報), Akechi Mitsuhide made several remarks that highlight how Yasuke was perceived in Japanese society. When Yasuke was captured, Mitsuhide reportedly said that Yasuke was "nothing more than a beast," or in other accounts, "a mere animal." The full quote from the Jesuit records roughly translates as:

"He is nothing more than a beast. He is not Japanese, so there is no need to kill him. Let the Jesuits have him."

This statement underscores several key points. Firstly, Yasuke's foreignness was a significant factor in how Mitsuhide viewed him—he was not seen as worthy of execution in the way that a samurai or high-ranking warrior might be, since captured samurai were usually swiftly executed especially by beheading. Secondly, The fact that he was spared is another significant point. Samurai captives of importance were often executed swiftly, and yet Yasuke was not only spared but was also sent to Kyōto's Nanban-dera (南蛮寺), the Jesuit mission. In this sense, Yasuke was treated more as a servant or foreign curiosity, rather than as a warrior deserving of respect.

DEBUNKING SENSATIONALIZED ACCOUNTS

In modern retellings, particularly in popular media, Yasuke is often depicted as a heroic figure who fought valiantly at Honnō-ji, resisting capture and embodying the code of the samurai. However, the historical reality is far less romantic. There is no record of Yasuke engaging in notable combat during the attack, and his immediate surrender further discredits the notion of him behaving as a samurai would in such a scenario.

The tendency to inflate Yasuke's role in the battle likely stems from a desire to align his story with familiar heroic tropes, such as that of the foreign warrior who earns a place of honor among the elite samurai. However, Yasuke's actual fate at Honnō-ji underscores the limitations of his status in Japan. His captors did not view him as a fellow warrior but rather as an exotic curiosity who had served Nobunaga as a retainer, not as a samurai.

Furthermore, the fact that Yasuke was sent back to the Jesuits after the battle suggests that he was not considered worthy of a warrior's execution or punishment. His connection to the Jesuits may have played a role in sparing his life, but this treatment reinforces the idea that Yasuke's place in Japanese society, while unique, was not as lofty as modern retellings would have us believe.

There is no historical record to support the claim that Yasuke took the head of Oda Nobunaga (織田信長) after Nobunaga's decapitation during the Battle of Honnō-ji (本能寺の変) and brought it back to Nobunaga's family. This narrative appears to be a later embellishment and lacks credible sources from the time.

THE VANISHING OF YASUKE FROM HISTORY

After being handed over to the Jesuits, Yasuke vanishes from historical records completely. There are no mentions of him in further Jesuit accounts, nor is he referenced in any other Japanese records after this point. This deafening silence in the historical record implies that Yasuke's role in Japan ended after Nobunaga's death and that he did not go on to live a life of significance in the public eye. Unlike many samurai and retainers of Nobunaga, whose fates were recorded after the battle, Yasuke simply fades from history, which further challenges any claim that he held a position of influence or status in Japan.

Many reports claim "'his performance on the battlefield and patrol duties were recognized, leading him to rise to the core of the samurai ranks' "but Jesuit *Japan Annual Report*, actually states that 'Nobunaga was greatly pleased with him, protected him, and assigned him a person to accompany him around the city.'

黒奴見物人の群集

復活祭日に続く週の月曜日〔三月二十七日、(十五日ヵ)〕信長は都に在たが、多数の人々がわが力ザの前に集って黒奴を見んとしたため騒が苦しく、投石のため負傷者を出し、また死せんとする者もあった。多数の人が門を衛ってみたにかかはらず、これを破ることを防ぐことは困難であった。もし金儲のために黒奴を観せ物としたらば、短期間に八千乃至一万クルサドを得ることは容易であらうと皆言った。

信長黒奴を観る

信長もこれを観んことを望んだ故、バードレ・オルガンチノが同人を連れて行った。大変な騒で、その色が自然であって人工でないことを信ぜず、常から上の着物を脱がせた。信長はまた彼等を抱いたが、その苦情に非常に喜んだ。今大坂の司令官である信長の甥もこれを観て非常に喜び、銭一万〔一貫ヵ〕〔文〕を与へた。

なる暴甚であるにかかはらず、当地方は数年来かつて見たることなき平和を楽しんである。バードレは黒奴一人を同伴してゐたが、都においてはかつて見たることなき故、諸人甚驚き、これを観んとして来た人は無数であった。信長自身もこれを観て驚き、生来の黒人で、墨を塗ったものでないことを容易に信ぜず、屡々これを親、少しく日本語を解したので、彼と話して鎧くことなく、また彼が力強く、少し

信長黒奴を飼る

の芸ができたので、信長は大いに喜んでこれを庄護し、人を附けて市内を巡らせた。彼を殿 Tono とするであらうと言ふ者もある。

またビジタドールが信長に贈った黒奴が、信長の死後此子の邸に赴き、相当長い間戦ってゐたところ、明智の家臣が

黒奴の銃

彼に近づいて、恐ることなくその刀を差出せと言ったのでこれを渡した。家臣はこの黒奴をいかに処分すべきか明智に尋ねたところ、黒奴は動物で何も知らず、また日本人でない故これを殺さず、インドのバードレの聖堂に置けと言った。これによって我等は少しく安心した。

二二四

A brief mention of Yasuke in 信長公記(*Shinchō Kōki*)

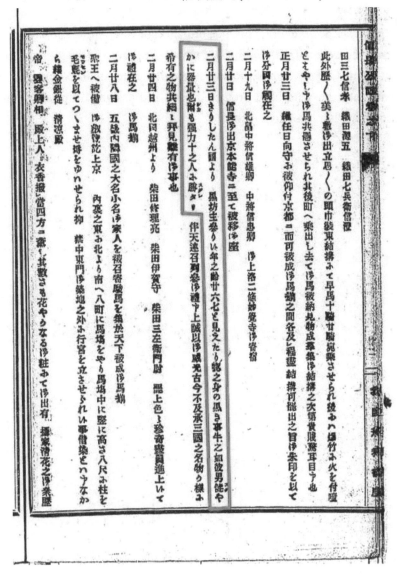

A brief mention of Yasuke in 家忠日記 (*Ietada Nikki*)

十二日戊辰　上様大さ御達成ニ五川成瓊病上気越ニ

十三日己巳　江戸立御成ニ濱松達城ニ

十四日庚午　田中守達病成ニ　みうら参達城ニ

十五日辛未　熊河立病成ニ

十六日壬申　濱松立病成中ニ

十七日癸酉　吉田達病成ニ　雨降

十八日甲戌　池程輔達病成中ニ　岳子へ行く

十九日乙亥　雨降　南澤　上様病成むらへ

つ是ニ御ニすきノヨトクメケハ六尺二あ尻ニ

南澤　上様病和吉ニ大シ参運五中ニらる男病

浄瑠トル

學鷹前池集二

The same book that records Yasuke's height also records the height of a mermaid.

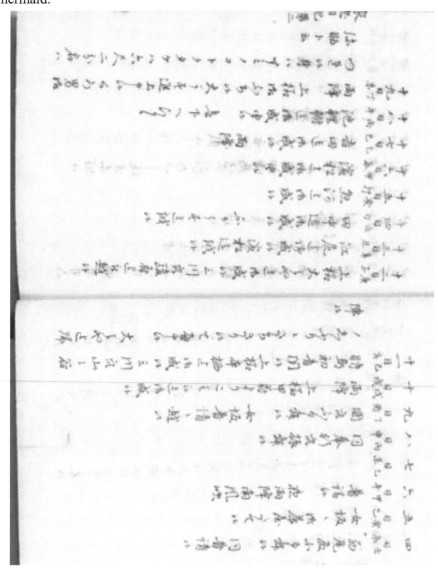

正月廿日ころん
てんぢくあがりに
あ五ミや金人をくいけ
参ハとのこゝ行ーと帰れ
せいハふな人二十名ハ
人魚云

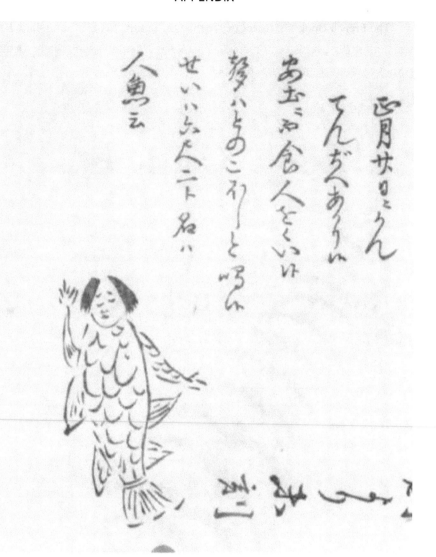

The French Book "Historie de l'eglise du japon" (1689) published 100 years after the events only records Yasuke as a "valet". This likely means he never attained any warrior rank.

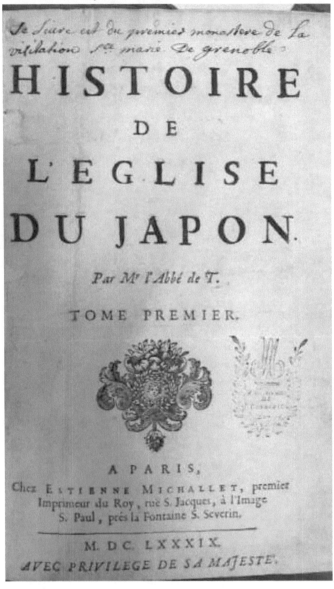

vint auſſi de Meaco & ils celebrerent la ſe-
maine Sainte avec toute la ſolemnité poſſible. On faiſoit tous les
jours un ſermon de la Paſſion de noſtre Seigneur, ou de l'inſtitu-
tion du ſaint Sacrement. Plus de quinze mille Chrétiens s'y aſ-
ſemblerent des lieux d'alentour, qui tous ſe confeſſerent & com-
munierent & pluſieurs d'entr'eux ſignalerent leur devotion par
des diſciplines ſanglantes.

Aprés les Feſtes de Paſques le Pere Valignam ſe tranſporta à
Meaco pour y faluër Nobunanga & pour le remercier des faveurs
continuelles qu'il répandoit ſur les Chrétiens & ſur les Peres qui
preſchoient dans ſon Royaume. Il avoit amené des Indes un
valet More. Auſſi-toſt qu'il parut dans la Ville tout le monde cou-
rut pour le voir. Le Pere Organtin le preſenta à Nobunanga,
qui en fut ſurpris & ne pouvoit croire que cette couleur fut na-
turelle: Mais il ſe perſuadoit qu'on l'avoit peint de la forte, ce qui
obligea le More de ſe dépoüiller juſqu'à la ceinture. Aprés l'avoir
bien examiné il en demeura convaincu. Il receut le Pere tres-fa-
vorablement & luy aſſigna un jour pour entretenir le Pere Vi-
ſiteur.

Le jour eſtant venu le P. Alexandre fut au Palais avec le Pere

"Imperial Dictionary" (Sanseido, 1896) 帝国大辞典」（三省堂、1896）shows that 「黒奴」was not a derogatory word.

こく-ど　名詞　(國土)　國の土地をいふ、「さ、くぢに安んず」など。

こく-ど　名詞　(國幣)　國庫の貨財をいふ。

こく-ど　名詞　(黑奴)　黑人を卑しめていふ語なり。

こくさう-とう　名詞　(黑頭公)　筆の異名なり。○「下學集」「黑頭公」。

こくさう-さう　名詞　(黑頭草)　うまきたしさいふ「におな」。

こくどの-かし　名詞　(黑頭草)　大戦の腦の植物にして、さらきの一名なり。

APPENDIX

Takaya Nakamura, "Modern Japanese History, Volume 2 (The Age of National Unity)" (Ikuei Shoin, 1917)中村孝也「日本近世史 第 2 巻 (国民統一の時代)」（育英書院、

1917 ） Records Yasuke as being a slave and that he danced for Nobunaga which Nobungaga found pleasing.

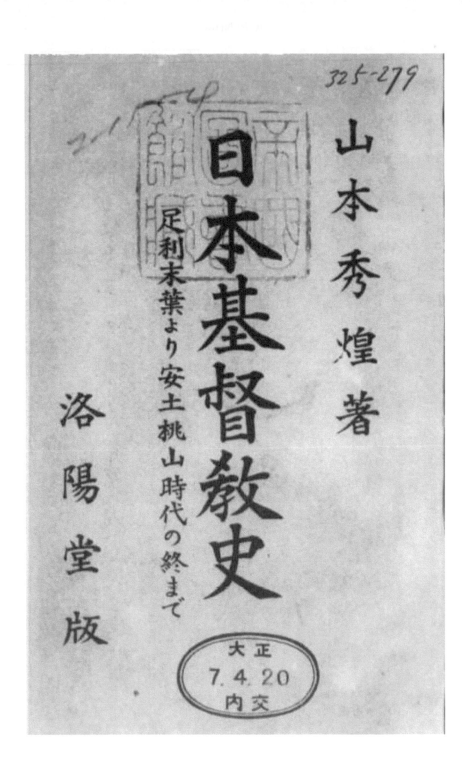

山本秀煌著

日本基督教史

足利末葉より安土桃山時代の終まで

洛陽堂版

信長黑奴 88 を見る

安土の學校

日本近世史

オルガンチノは謁見のとき、孔雀、遠目鏡、伽羅、虎皮、八疊つりの蚊張蝿々緋の巻物、藥種、頗野牛、羊、唐犬等を獻じて信長の歡心を求めしが、信長を最も悅ばしたるは、黑奴なりき。『信長記』に曰く、「二月二十三日天正九年、きりしたん國より黑坊參候。年の齡二十六七と見へたり。惣の身體黑き事如牛。彼男健やかに器量なり。剛も强力十人に勝れたり。伴天連召連參御禮申上」と。

この黑奴はこの年高槻にて舉行せる基督其天祭に當り、舞踏を演じ、一萬五千の會衆をして喝采せしめしもの也。師父ワリニャノ之を伴ひて京都に入り、信長に謁せしに、信長は、皮膚の黑きを驚き、衣を脱して半身を顯はさしめ仔細に點檢して初めて真の皮膚なるを信じたりと傳ふ。

信長は天正七年、オルガンチノを引見し安土に僧院及び會堂を建つることを許し、宮殿に面し、山と町との間にある入江を埋め、二十日にして其工を了り、埋立地及鄰接せる二軒の家屋の敷地を宣敎師に興たり。ついて天正九年アレキサンデル、ワリニャノ(Alexander Valignani)の請ひにより學校を立てしめ、オルガンチノをその主宰たらしむ。こゝにおいて彼等は數年前京

243

Steichen. M (1910) THE CHRISTIAN DAIMYOS. A Century of
Religious and Political History in Japan. (1549-1650.) Rikkyo Gakuin
Press, Tokyo- Mentions only one black man was spared in the Honnoji
Incident

Chapitre VI.

Le soir même, Akechi retourne à Kyōto, et le lendemain matin, de
très bonne heure, ses hommes sont devant les portes de la ville,
attendant le signal de l'attaque: Ce signal donné, ils envahissent la
ville et se précipitent sur le Honnō-ji, temple où Nobunaga avait
établi sa demeure. Celui-ci venait de se lever, quand tout à coup il
entend du tumulte et des détonations d'arquebuse dans la cour.
Brusquement il ouvre une des portes roulantes, mais aussitôt une
grêle de flèches lui sont décochées. Blessé à l'épaule, il retire lui-
même la flèche, et s'armant de son sabre fond sur les agresseurs.
Mais bientôt, atteint d'un coup d'arquebuse, il est obligé de se
retirer à l'intérieur du temple. Il a encore la force de refermer la
porte, et tombe pour ne plus se relever. Ses serviteurs accourus à
son secours se donnent la mort, et couvrent de leurs cadavres le
corps de leur maître.

Au même instant, le feu éclate en plusieurs endroits et consume le
temple avec tous ceux qui s'y trouvent. Seul le nègre, que les
religieux avaient abandonné à Nobunaga, échappe à la catastrophe
et se réfugie dans la maison des Jésuites. Nobutada, fils aîné de
Nobunaga, occupait le temple Myokaku-ji. En apprenant la
trahison d'Akechi, il court au Honnō-ji avec Murai, le gouverneur
de la ville. Mais à la vue du temple entièrement enveloppé de
flammes, tous deux se retirent au palais de Nijō, où, attaqués par
les troupes d'Akechi, ils font le hara-kiri. Telle fut la fin tragique
de Nobunaga, le mercredi, 22 juin 1582.

ENGLISH TRANSLATION:

Chapter VI.

That same evening, Akechi returns to Kyoto, and early the next morning, his men are positioned in front of the city gates, waiting for the signal to attack. Once the signal is given, they invade the city and rush toward Honnō-ji, the temple where Nobunaga had established his residence. Nobunaga had just risen when he suddenly heard tumult and the sound of arquebus shots in the courtyard. He quickly opens one of the sliding doors, but is immediately struck by a hail of arrows. Wounded in the shoulder, he pulls the arrow out himself and, armed with his sword, charges at his attackers. But soon, struck by an arquebus shot, he is forced to retreat inside the temple. He still has the strength to close the door but falls, never to rise again. His servants rush to his aid, only to take their own lives, covering their master's body with their corpses.

At the same time, fires break out in several places, consuming the temple along with everyone inside. Only the black man, whom the religious figures had left with Nobunaga, escapes the catastrophe and seeks refuge in the Jesuit house. Nobutada, Nobunaga's eldest son, was occupying the Myōkaku-ji temple. Upon learning of Akechi's betrayal, he rushes to Honnō-ji with Murai, the governor of the city. But seeing the temple completely engulfed in flames, both withdraw to the Nijō Palace, where, attacked by Akechi's troops, they commit hara-kiri. Such was the tragic end of Nobunaga, on Wednesday, June 22, 1582.

In this sense the "escape" refers to escaping with his life since we know that he was captured by Mistuhide.

Le soir même, Akechi retourne à Kyôto, et le lendemain matin, de très bonne heure, ses hommes
sont devant les portes de la ville, attendant le signal de l'attaque. Ce signal donné, ils envahissent
la ville et se précipitent sur le Honnô-ji, temple où
Nobunaga avait établi sa demeure. Celui-ci venait
de se lever, quand tout à coup il entend du tumulte
et des détonations d'arquebuse dans la cour. Brusquement il ouvre une des portes roulantes, mais
aussitôt une grêle de flèches lui sont décochées.
Blessé à l'épaule, il retire lui-même la flèche, et
s'armant de son sabre fond sur les agresseurs. Mais
bientôt, atteint d'un coup d'arquebuse, il est obligé
de se retirer à l'intérieur du temple. Il a encore la
force de refermer la porte, et tombe pour ne plus
se relever. Ses serviteurs accourus à son secours se
donnent la mort, et couvrent de leurs cadavres le
corps de leur maître.

Au même instant, le feu éclate en plusieurs endroits et consume le temple avec tous ceux qui s'y
trouvent. Seul le nègre, que les religieux avaient
abandonné à Nobunaga, échappe à la catastrophe
et se réfugie dans la maison des Jésuites. Nobutada,
fils aîné de Nobunaga, occupait le temple Miyo-
kaku-ji. En apprenant la trahison d'Akechi, il court
au Honnô-ji avec Murai, le gouverneur de la ville.
Mais à la vue du temple entièrement enveloppé de
flammes, tous deux se retirent au palais de Nijô, où,
attaqués par les troupes d'Akechi, ils font le hara-
kiri. Telle fut la fin tragique de Nobunaga, le mercredi, 22 juin 1582.

PORTUGUESE JESUIT DOCUMENT 1581

TRANSCRIPTION (PORTUGUESE):

"... era a gente que o vinha ver que não tinha conto, & o mesmo Nobunanga pasmou de o ver nem se podia persuadir que naturalmente era negro, mas que era artificio de tinta, & assi não se fartava de o ver muitas vezes, & falar com elle, porque sabia mediocremente a lingua de Japão, & tinha muitas forças, & algumas manhas boas, de que elle muito gustava, agora o favorece tanto que o mandou por toda a cidade com hum homem seu muito privado pera que todos soubessem que elle o amava: dizem que o fará Tõno."

TRANSLATION (ENGLISH):

"... the people who came to see him were countless, and Nobunaga himself was astonished to see him, unable to believe that he was naturally black, thinking instead that it was the work of paint, and thus he couldn't get enough of seeing him many times and speaking with him, because he had a moderate grasp of the Japanese language, and he had great strength and some good skills, which Nobunaga liked very much. Now he favors him so much that he sent him around the city with one of his most trusted men so that everyone would know that he loved him: they say he will make him a Tono (Lord)."

foi vifto no ſarao; e a palmai a to
dos, era a gente que o vinha ver q̃
não tinha conto, & o meſmo Nobu
ninga palmou de o ver nem ſe podia perſuadir que naturalmente e.
ra negro, mas que era artificio de
tinta, & aſsi não ſe fartaua de o ver
muitas vezes, & falar com elle, por
que ſabia mediocremente a lingoa
de Iapaõ, & tinha muitas forças, &
algũas manhas boas, de que elle
muito goſtaua, agora o fauorece
tanto que o mandou por toda a cidade com hũm homem ſeu muito
priuado pera que todos ſoubeſſem
que elle o amaua: dizem que o fa-
râ Tòno. Ordenou mais o padre
em Anzuquíyama hum ſeminario
de alguns vinte & cinco mininos Ia
pões de muito boa abilidade, & en
genho que aprendẽ a ler, & eſcre-

信長公記 Honnoji Incident (Nobunaga Koki) 信長公記の
699 ページより

Listing men who died in the incident. Full text at :
https://kokusho.nijl.ac.jp/biblio/100108970/699?ln=ja

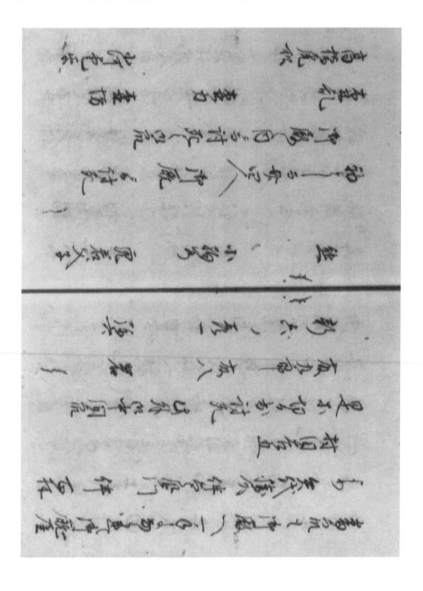

FURTHER WORKS

Original 家忠日記

https://dl.ndl.go.jp/pid/1885131/1/1

Saint Francis Xavier and the Roots of Christianity in Japan
https://www.nippon.com/en/features/c02303/

丹波亀山鉄炮隊
Luis Frois
https://tk-teppou.com/kawaraban/luis_frois.html

Lourenco Mexia
https://www.redalyc.org/pdf/361/36112010004.pdf

大道寺友山. (1685). 武道初心集.
https://books.google.co.kr/books?id=O5RXAAAAcAAJ&printsec=f
rontcover&redir_esc=y#v=onepage&q&f=false

Made in United States
Troutdale, OR
11/07/2024

24547678R00139